One Nation Under God *is an in̄ṭẹḷḷịg̣ẹ̣ṇṭ, p̣...*
researched call to action for Christians to stand up and be
counted. Cynthia brilliantly clears a direct path between
Biblical principles and the foundation of our Government.
A must read.

—Jennifer O'Neill,
Model, Actress, Author and Speaker

If you dare to open your eyes and truly understand where
this nation is headed, read this book!

-Bill Wilson
The Daily Jot News Service

This book is like a kick-in-the-gut, wake up call. It made me
more aware, and angry at my own apathy.

—Rick Heil
Lead Singer, Sonic Flood

Jesus once lamented that the children of this world are often
wiser than the children of light. This book helps reverse that,
showing us how to influence every aspect of society.

—Dave Barton
President of Wallbuilders and
author of numerous historical books

ONE
NATION

UNDER
GOD

ONE
NATION

UNDER
GOD

Cynthia Noland Dunbar, Esq.

One Nation Under God by Cynthia Noland Dunbar, Esq.

Published by Onward, an imprint of HigherLife Development Services, Inc.
2342 Westminster Terrace
Oviedo, Florida 32765
407-563-4806
www.ahigherlife.com

Unless otherwise noted Scripture quotations are from the New King James Version of the Bible. Copyright © 1979, 1980, 1982 by Thomas Nelson, Inc., publishers. Used by permission.

Cover Design: Think Agency

ISBN 978-0-9793227-2-3

Printed in the United States of America

Dedication

This book is dedicated to my entire family, but most especially to my parents who have always been there for me and always believed in me, my sister who has actively promoted me and this book, and to my two precious children who, aside from Christ, are my greatest treasure. Thank you, thank you, thank you!

TABLE OF CONTENTS

———⟫●⟪———

Without God, there is no virtue, because there's no prompting of the conscience. Without God, we're mired in the material, that flat world that tells us only what the senses perceive. Without God, there is a coarsening of the society. And without God, democracy will not and cannot long endure. *If we ever forget that we're one nation under God, then we will be a nation gone under.*

—President Ronald Reagan
Dallas, Texas
August 23, 1984

———⟫●⟪———

PREFACE

HIS BOOK IS A MUST-READ FOR EVERY
Christian who sincerely desires to have an
impact on the world. We are all called to take
the gospel of Christ and infuse it into society. I am not
merely speaking of evangelizing our neighbors. Our
scope of influence needs to be much broader than that.
The Father definitely wants us to lead others to a saving
knowledge of Jesus Christ, but He also wants us to be salt
and light in every activity and realm of daily living. When
He commanded us to take the gospel to the nations, I
believe He meant more by that than to simply send out
missionaries. I believe He meant "the Nations" as in all
peoples and all governments. Is it in knowing Christ
as Sovereign and Creator of all governing authorities

that gives meaning to the government being upon His shoulders? When we pray, "thy Kingdom come, thy will be done on earth as it is in heaven," are we accountable to include governments and rulers?

I am convinced our Founding Fathers were keenly aware of this lofty obligation. They took seriously their stand for liberty and freedom because they understood the immense responsibility they faced. They were entrusted with the task of constructing a government that would help direct human affairs in such a way as to acknowledge God's kingdom principles here on earth.

An old adage states that if America ceases to be good, she will cease to be great, and it is true. But what the adage underestimates is the subtlety the enemy would use to cause the salt of goodness to lose its savor, or more pointedly, its realm of influence. The body of Christ was gradually lulled into complacency. We took ourselves out of both the political and social arenas to sit silently in our pews. These decades of apathy have cost us as a nation a great deal. Many, if not most, of our Constitutional freedoms and liberties have been sacrificed on the altar of social evolution. We have bought into the lies of the prevailing will of the masses as though we were a pure democracy. We have accepted our plight when our elected officials tell us they are bound to follow the will of the people, even when such will is a direct assault upon the Constitution.

It is time the body of Christ in the United States was reminded of who we as a nation truly are. We are not, nor have we ever been, a pure democracy. We are a Republic, one nation under God, with liberty and justice for all, and those elected to hold public office have a sworn oath to uphold the Constitution in all of its biblically-derived principles. We can't preserve our government unless we understand it and diligently fight to protect it. It is the goal of this book and the hope of its author that those reading these pages will fervently grasp the biblical function of civil government as it was envisioned by our Founding Fathers. Such understanding will inevitably birth the vision of being social-change agents, enacting the principles of God's kingdom on earth. The need is great; the time is now.

This book is more than a historical review, more than a simple documentary. It hopefully rises to the level of a rebirth of ideals. Our Founding Fathers did not concoct a set of values and principles on which to base the Constitution; rather they were the first to fully implement those standards once generally accepted as the Laws of Nature and of Nature's God. The principles espoused within these Laws of Nature find their source in divine law. Consequently, the underlying authority for our constitutional form of government stems directly from biblical precedents. Hence, the only accurate method of ascertaining the intent of the Founding Fathers at the time of our government's inception comes from a biblical worldview. This is not a statement of intolerance. It is a statement of fact. I am aware that such a politically incorrect statement will be characterized as that of a narrow-minded, right-wing zealot. However, truth is truth and it cannot be altered or swayed by social acceptance or belief. It is past time for the church in America to stop hiding and denying the rich past we enjoy as a nation and to start demanding civil accountability to this truth. It is my prayer that this book will serve as a wake-up call to the church of the United States of America.

I realize many may view this book as highly controversial; truth almost always is. Therefore, the following chapters are not intended for the faint-at-heart or the apathetic, the complacent or the deceived. However, my intent is not to shock but rather to present facts, allowing them to both inform and convict. Hopefully such conviction will eliminate the comfort of a middle-of-the road approach to civic involvement. The black-or-white choice we unknowingly confront every day will become eminently clear. To read it is to come face-to-face with the reality that there are no legitimate defenses to the church abdicating its role within society. While we have been complacent in our ignorance, there has been a strategic, methodical and unrelenting assault upon our nation's heritage by humanistic special-interest groups. They are militant in their attacks to remove God from the public square. If we fail to enter the battle, we will lose our place in the world as One Nation Under God and will be forevermore One Nation gone Under!

Chapter One

DISCERNING
THE TIMES

⊶•⊷

D
O YOU HAVE ANY IDEA WHAT TIME IT IS?"
I am not referring to the time indicated on
your watch or cell phone. The real question is, "Do you discern the times in which we find
ourselves?" A question a dear friend used to contem-
plate is, "What do you think was going through the
minds of the majority of German Jews immediately
prior to the Holocaust?" The reality is, there were signs
of things to come in their increasingly demoralized

society. However, it seems most likely, considering the absence of a mass exodus, that the majority could not conceive of anything so horrific as what would come. Surely, it was incomprehensible that such atrocities could take place, at least not in the modern and civilized day and country in which they lived.

The similarities to our own country are striking. Both societies increasingly embraced the merits of quality of life over sanctity of life, or the belief that certain human beings did not merit the protection of the laws. A judiciary legislating without restraint, an education system promoting moral relativism and natural selection as unquestionable truths, and a media framing the country's issues and leaders in the kind of light that socialistic elites desiring a strong centralized government would like—all are effective tools for nurturing tyranny. The most significant similarity, however, is the unwillingness of the targeted group of people to accept that they are the unfortunate "chosen people." In America today that would be the devout, Bible-believing Christians.

Okay, you think I am being paranoid. Then name one group of individuals whom it is acceptable to malign other than Bible-believing, sincere followers of Christ? And what about leadership? Well, I guess that is the one missing ingredient. After all, we certainly lack a charismatic, driven leader with a hidden agenda, a leader who comes out of nowhere who seems to command the awe and allegiance of many. Or are we? The bottom line is that it is the state of moral decay in the people, not the existence or absence of such a leader, that opens the door to societies such as pre-Holocaust Germany. The Scripture tells us that when the righteous are in power the people rejoice, but when the wicked are in power the people mourn (Prov. 29:2). I no longer believe this refers to a single leader in power. Our leaders, especially in America, are merely a reflection of the hearts and desires of the people who elect them. When godly, moral people predominate in a culture, they will select like-minded leaders. Consequently, the state in which our nation currently finds itself is more a reflection of the state of moral decline of our general populace than it is a reflection of the lack of true moral leadership. This lack seems to stem from the absence of any meaningful input from strict adherents of the Word of God, historically, the guiding light of our nation to greatness. How has this transpired?

A recent article in the *Seattle Times* discusses a trend among younger so-called "evangelicals" not to be governed by the one or two family issues that drove prior generations into the Republican camp. The article attempts to explain the leveling of competition between the two parties due to the fact the Democratic Party allegedly has the Christian edge on issues such as AIDS in Africa, poverty, and social justice. My response to this comment is simply this: *seriously*? Christians who truly possess a biblical worldview would know better than to buy into the lie that the Democratic position on even these issues aligns with Scripture; clearly, it does not.

The biblical worldview, or the mindset that is based upon a clear application of scripture, understands that civil government is to have no involvement or jurisdiction over the realm of benevolence or aid to the poor. First of all, a heart-felt conviction or desire to aid our fellow man is one governed by the first amendment as our free exercise of our personal rights. I will discuss and detail this jurisdictional understanding more fully later in this book. However, the government has no right to coerce aid contrary to the dictates of one's conscience. Additionally, the role of aid to the poor is scripturally defined to lie within the purview of religion and is not a role for the civil government to play. So, while the Christian position is clearly one of being moved with compassion to meet the needs of those less fortunate than we are, the belief in the reapportionment of wealth through government action comes not from a biblical worldview but from a socialistic and even communistic one.

Need I continue? As for social justice, what types of issues do they want to ambiguously lump together in their futile arguments that such align with biblical principles? Hate crimes, perhaps? Hate crimes legislation is a frightening and dangerous tool that in no way finds its underpinnings in biblical law. First of all, there are already on the books numerous punishments for violent and offensive crimes such as assault and murder. Second, the only two options for justifying these laws demand that either the courts give preferred status to certain victims or our citizenry can now be punished not merely for their actions but because of their thoughts or what is in their hearts. Obviously, no one would ever dare to admit that the intent of such laws was to give an unconstitutional preference to a select group of people. Therefore, the only argument remaining is that these additional penalties are occasioned by the desire to govern what is in the hearts of man. Now, while I in absolutely no way condone or even understand the type of hatefulness certain individuals harbor, hatefulness that would lead to such heinous and despicable crimes, it is their actions alone, not their hearts, over which the civil government is biblically allowed to exercise jurisdiction. The Bible is very clear from I Samuel 16:7, Acts 15:8, and Revelations 2:23 as to the single individual who possesses jurisdiction over our hearts, and it is not the civil authorities. When any government has usurped authority over the hearts of its people, it has always led to a very oppressive society.

So why is the Democratic position on these issues drawing so-called evangelicals under the age of 35? Again, there can only be two options. Either the church in America has become so ignorant of the principles espoused within the Word of God or these "evangelicals" are not really who they say they are. Perhaps it

5

is easier to lead certain Christians astray when they believe they are aligning with other like-minded individuals. Either way, we are headed for disaster unless these misperceptions are exposed.

How did we get where we are and where are we really? We are living in a generation where untold thousands of people are willing to check their personal beliefs at the polling booth to justify supporting candidates whose basic policies are diametrically opposed to the word of God. We are living in a day and age where even the seeming devout are willing to compromise their faith to find a reason to exempt their political and social alliances from compliance with their professed faith. I have seen websites and blogs where a certain presidential candidate is referred to as a Messiah. As sincere Christians, these statements should be blasphemous to us. The Word tells us in Matthew 24:24 that in the end there will appear false prophets who will deceive even the very elect,. Well apparently, there are numerous people deceived. What I find disturbing is that few are speaking out about the precarious position in which we find ourselves as a nation. And while we are called not to judge, we are also told to be discerning and watch out for those who are not true followers of Christ. Matthew 7:15-21 shows us that we are called to weigh the fruit and actions of a person's life to see if they truly are doing the will of the Father. This responsibility to discern would seem to be essential in the selection of our leadership. Yet, in spite of voting records and speeches clearly espousing non-biblical standards, Christians are swayed like sheep by rhetoric and media hype. In order to do so, they must first delude themselves into accepting that these two divergent positions are not mutually exclusive. To that deception I simply must reply, oh, but they are.

What I am describing is a blatant disconnect between a personal profession of or belief in the Word coupled with a failure or ignorance in knowing how to carry out Biblical principles within the framework of our society. There are fewer places this is seen so clearly as in what is known as the emergent church and its propensity for alignment within the political realm. The following is a quote from an article in Christianity Today from a leader in the emergent church discussing the politics of many within its following.

> ... [T]he emerging movement is a latte-drinking, backpack-lugging, Birkenstock-wearing group of 21st-century, left-wing, hippie wannabes. Put directly, they are Democrats. And that spells 'post' for conservative-evangelical-politics-as-usual. I have publicly aligned myself with the emerging movement. What attracts me is its soft postmodernism (or critical realism) and its praxis/missional focus. I also lean left in

politics. I tell my friends that I have voted Democrat for years for all the wrong reasons. I don't think the Democratic Party is worth a hoot, but its historic commitment to the poor and to centralizing government for social justice is what I think government should do. I don't support abortion—in fact, I think it is immoral. I believe in civil rights, but I don't believe homosexuality is God's design. And, like many in the emerging movement, I think the Religious Right doesn't see what it is doing.[1]

While I will concede that many within the Religious Right may not see what we are doing, I find it very telling that the same two examples of poverty and social justice are used to attempt to justify this political association. I suppose this serves to only further underscore my point that in order to embrace such positions, one must first abandon a desire for strict adherence to biblical principles, or at least an understanding and practical application of them. I do not know anyone within the emergent church and I am not questioning their sincerity, but such arguments involving the biblical position on poverty and social issues does not align with the Democratic Party's positions on these issues. Such arguments can only be effective where there is a true ignorance of the Word of God. We, as the body of Christ must regain a love for the Word as is described in Psalms 119 and this love of the Word will enable us to stay the course. In short, if the Word is Christ, and Christ is God, then the Word is God. And to embrace anything other than the Word is to embrace a deity other than the one true God. Therefore, to live your life following such beliefs is to walk in a form of idolatry. Nothing should ever be allowed to take precedence over our allegiance to our Savior and to the general principles of Christianity.

Second president John Adams wrote to Thomas Jefferson that America's independence arose from the Founding Fathers' commitment to "the general principles of Christianity." He went on to say that, "those general principles of Christianity are as eternal and immutable as the existence and attributes of God; and that those principles of liberty are as unalterable as human nature."[2] Whoever would instill into the affairs of mankind the basic principles of Christianity will forever change the face of the earth.[3] That is, in truth, what our Founding Fathers did. Their system of government worked not because they were brilliant, although many of them were. The government worked so effectively because it was based upon underlying, eternal, and immutable truths that, if implemented, do work. Now, our nation stands at the precipice of turning its back on these underlying principles, and it doesn't take either a political analyst or a prophet to predict that our government will not long stand outside this framework.

We can therefore see the proverbial handwriting on the wall, which, by the way, is a phrase whose origination came from the Holy Scriptures. In Daniel, the hand of God proclaimed a judgment by writing a prophetic declaration on the wall because of the rebellion and obstinacy of His people.[4] Well, we have a similar warning that is confronting us glaringly; the only issue is, do we have eyes to see it or ears to hear it?

Many do not, but for those of us who do, we are ill-equipped to apply the Founders intentions unless we understand their framework for the pre-existence of law. We have heard it said that we should return to the Faith of our founding fathers? I would say such a statement, while well intentioned, is too limiting. Yes, we must return to their faith, but only to the extent that they were truly successful in implementing the civil society they intended.

Chapter Two

THE PRE-EXISTENCE
OF LAW

———⇒●⇐———

H OW MANY TIMES HAVE WE HEARD WE
should return to the beliefs of our Founding
Fathers? If all we are doing is returning to
subjective beliefs held by mortal—albeit awe-inspiring—
men, then we need not bother. However, I do believe
we should return to the beliefs of our Founding Fathers,
and that is because our Founding Fathers put their
hope and faith in something much larger and much
more trustworthy than their own individual opinions.

In order to understand what it was they believed and how much larger those beliefs were than themselves, we must look to the authors they were reading at the time of our nation's founding.

Where, for example, did the Founders get their idea for three separate branches: the judicial, the legislative, and the executive? Did they create this form of civil government or were they merely the first to fully implement it? Why did they believe it was crucial we have a system of checks and balances? In order to answer these questions and more about what the Founders sincerely intended in their creation of our constitutional form of government, one must glean an accurate understanding of their underlying beliefs.

To most effectively accomplish this, we must look to those to whom the Founders looked to develop their understanding of civil authority. Roughly ninety-four percent of all quotes of the Founding Fathers at the time of America's founding were either directly or indirectly from the Bible. When I say indirectly, I simply mean these men quoted other individuals, who, in turn, had quoted the Bible. A careful reading of such documents as the Federalist Papers, the Anti-Federalist Papers—as well as our founding documents, the Declaration of Independence, the Articles of Confederation, and the Constitution—reveal certain underlying principles espoused by other authors. In identifying these authors we soon discover who were the three thinkers heavily relied on by our Founders. The third most-quoted individual was the English philosopher John Locke. The second most-quoted was the celebrated English jurist Sir William Blackstone, and the most-quoted was the French political thinker Baron de Montesquieu. To read these authors' writings, which were fairly contemporaneous to our country's founding, is to obtain a clear vision of the underlying belief systems our Founders possessed concerning civil jurisdiction.

The third most-quoted individual by the Founders was John Locke. His in-depth and extensive analysis of the rule of law—especially in his *Two Treatises of Government*, published in 1690—was obviously an inspiration to those charting our nation's birth. Locke proclaimed that *"The Law of Nature stands as an eternal rule to all men, legislators as well as others. The rules that they make for other men's actions must...be conformable to the Law of Nature...."* He then defined the Law of Nature as the will of God.

In his second treatise, called *On Civil Government,* Locke further explained his philosophy as to the appropriateness of and foundation for man-made law. He referred to a quote from theologian Richard Hooker's *Ecclesiastical Polity:* "Human Laws are measures in respect of Men whose actions they must direct...such measures...have...their higher Rules to be measured by, which Rules are 2, the Law of God, and the Law of Nature; so that laws Human must be made according to the general Laws of Nature, and without contradiction to any positive Law of scripture, otherwise they are ill made."[5]

From this single author, we can glean that he clearly accepted and was promoting government on the basis of a biblical worldview. All right, you say, but Locke was only the third most-quoted philosopher. Let's then look at the second most-quoted individual. Sir William Blackstone published his *Commentaries on the Laws of England* between 1765 and 1769. Obviously his writings were very timely, affording serious review by the Founders.

Locke agreed with a bold statement concerning what constitutes appropriate human laws, that they "... must be made according to the general Laws of Nature, and without contradiction to any positive Law of scripture, otherwise they are ill made." Surely Blackstone, writing eighty-six years later, would take a more moderate and, as we say today, "politically correct" position. Well, if that is what you were hoping to find, you would be greatly disappointed. Blackstone actually took a more aggressive position on the validity of human laws, saying essentially that "Law is not law if it is contrary to the laws of nature and of nature's God." Blackstone made the jump from Locke's simply calling such laws "ill made" to actually proclaiming them as null and void. His position was that such laws are without effect if they are made outside the standard of compliance with the will of God, ascertainable by the Holy Scriptures.

For those readers still holding out that all they've been taught about our Founders' deist viewpoints that supported a philosophy of separation of church and state is true, we have one author still to examine, the one quoted by the Founders more than any other. The individual most quoted by the framers of our great nation was Charles-Louis Joseph de Secondat, Baron de Montesquieu. Montesquieu was a Frenchman whose discourse on the authority of law was set down in *The Spirit of Laws* in 1748. In this manuscript Montesquieu explained his belief in the appropriateness of three branches of government and documents that such philosophy originated in Isaiah 33:22. "For the Lord is our Judge, the Lord is our Lawgiver, and the Lord is our King." This was his basis for suggesting the judicial, legislative, and executive branches of civil authority.

Additionally, the Baron ascertained the need for checks and balances due to his assessment of the basic nature of mankind. Essentially, he agreed with the Scriptures, which tell us that "the heart is deceitful above all things, and desperately wicked: who can know it?" (Jer. 17:9). For Montesquieu, it was this understanding of the shortcomings or fallen nature of man that made selfless and circumspect leadership doubtful at best. Inserting checks and balances into our system of government, thereby making all three branches accountable to the rule of law, was not a creative attempt at framing a new form of Republic. Rather, Montesquieu considered it a remedy to address the concern that mankind left to itself was incapable of selfless and altruistic governing. These beliefs and assumptions, presented within *The Spirit of Laws,* clearly document the biblical worldview possessed by Montesquieu.

In reviewing quotes of the Founding Fathers, scholars have estimated that approximately thirty-four percent are taken directly from the Holy Bible. This is, therefore, the most frequently quoted manuscript. However, in reviewing all citations, including both indirect and direct quotes, indirect being quotes taken from other prior authors such as Locke, Blackstone, and Montesquieu, who themselves quoted or referenced scripture, the total has been estimated to be approximately ninety-four percent. That is much more than a simple majority. If any candidate in today's society received a ninety-four percent approval rating, they would take it as more than a mandate; they would be convinced they held the hearts and minds of the American public. The percentage is such an overwhelming figure that there can be no doubt that, in the words of the Supreme Court's opinion in *Holy Trinity Church v. United States* (1892), "our government and our institutions are emphatically Christian."[6]

The importance of understanding the underlying framework for the establishment of a new government in our nation cannot be minimized. It shows clearly that the drafters of our Declaration and Constitution grasped and adhered to a belief in the pre-existence of law prior to any law established by men. This belief system declares that all laws and all systems of laws derived their validity and authority from their alignment with the principles of Holy Scripture and the will of the Supreme Creator of the Universe. Such a belief system would, consequently, require that any person desiring to govern have a sincere knowledge and appreciation for the Word of God in order to rightly govern. I realize that such a truth will most certainly be offensive to those who find Christianity abhorrent, those who desire the passage of laws that do not align with Scripture, and those who deny the very existence of a Creator God. However, truth is truth irrespective of who believes it. Every student everywhere may be convinced that $2 + 2 = 5$, but this majority opinion does not in any way diminish or impair the truth that the correct answer is 4.

C.S. Lewis, the Oxford don who is better known these days for his Chronicles of Narnia, was a brilliant apologist and logician. The following quotes frame the futility of arguing against truth and truth has a name, the name of Jesus Christ. Lewis writes, in *Mere Christianity,* "When you are arguing against Him you are arguing against the very power that makes you able to argue at all." In *An Experiment in Criticism,* he argues, "A man can no more diminish God's glory by refusing to worship Him than a lunatic can put out the sun by scribbling the word 'darkness' on the walls of his cell." And from the same work, Lewis goes on to say, "In coming to understand anything we are rejecting the facts as they are for us in favour of the facts as they are." In order for those who oppose the Christian faith to embrace the truth that America was founded with an emphatically Christian government, they must first be willing to reject the facts they perceive to be in their favor in exchange for what the facts simply are.

Where does this leave us? We have a nation whose Founders intended to establish it squarely on the foundation of biblical truth. This is a very significant realization. Anyone sincerely wishing to argue from where our civil authority is derived, no longer may use as the basis for their argument merely what the Founders may have said or done. George Washington himself adroitly predicted the inevitability of his own error and consequently prayed for the Lord to lessen the effects of such mistakes. "Though, in reviewing the incidents of my Administration, I am unconscious of intentional error, I am nevertheless too sensible of my defects not to think it probable that I may have committed many errors. Whatever they may be I fervently beseech the Almighty to avert or mitigate the evils to which they may tend."[7] It must therefore be Washington's and his colleagues' underlying intention to follow the will of God that should ultimately direct our future actions, not their ability to have performed perfectly all they had intended to accomplish.

Following the Founders' commitment to God's law and the Scriptures, which reveal that law, it becomes clear that in order to be knowledgeable in the proper implementation of public policy, one must not only have the ability to interpret biblical principles but also be able to apply those principles. This is where those who governed our nation strived to exist for almost two hundred years. However, the nation veered dangerously off course when those equipped to understand and implement these principles stepped out of the realm of public influence. Those called to be salt and light were failing to be salty, and they certainly were not casting a high-beam of direction for our nation. Those whom the Lord had called righteous in accord with II Corinthians 5:21 had bought into the subtle lies of keeping the church inside the four walls of the church. This abdication from civic involvement has taken a tragic toll on the moral health of our nation as a whole, as well as the individual lives of its inhabitants. The truth that God has called us as Christians to be in the world but not of the world was transformed into the lie that we were not to be salt and light. Adding a little truth to a perversion is a very dangerous thing, as C.S. Lewis notes in *The Last Battle,* the last book of his Chronicles. Jill Pole sees through the designs of Narnia's enemies: "And then she understood the devilish cunning of the enemies' plan.

By mixing a little truth with it they had made their lie far stronger."

Having seen our Founding Fathers' reverence for and use of biblical truth, there can be no doubt that we are a nation founded upon biblical truths, truths that are eternal and immutable. Nonetheless, we find ourselves constantly battling the onslaught of godlessness and immorality, all under the guise of tolerance and social evolution. With this clear understanding of the Laws of Nature and of Nature's God, how is it that we have gotten so far away from being a Judeo-Christian nation? How did we essentially lose our identity? The primary blame belongs to one group of people, but it is not likely the group to whom we would like to ascribe responsibility.

Chapter Three

Abdication of the Righteous Right

<hr/>

T HE UNITED STATES OF AMERICA HAS
a history rich with ideals, ideals that provide
the framework for our nation. The Declaration
of Independence makes clear that mankind has "inalienable rights" to "life, liberty, and the pursuit of happiness."
But the ideals of life and liberty have been trampled
underfoot by a perverted concept of the pursuit of
happiness. The price we paid for the sin of slavery was
devastatingly high. Abortion remains a blight upon

our land, the price for which we have yet to pay. Can we even begin to fathom the penalty for the rampant destruction of innocent life that has gone unchecked for so long? Sexual promiscuity is not only allowed, but it is condoned and even lauded as normal. Homosexual relationships are likewise flaunted by anti-family propaganda, and now the Courts have gone so far as to allow for homosexual marriage, an institution that has been said to never before have been acknowledged other than in the days of Noah. Our nation has gone from a beacon of morality and decency to one of debauchery and licentiousness. The only liberties disdained by our society have become those of piety and holiness. Truly the shame should weigh heavily upon us.

Who bears the responsibility for this shame? Is it the unredeemed, who seek to silence the church in an effort to justify any course of action they desire to take? Is it the social elite, who seek to rewrite our history in an effort to erase any semblance of religion and morality as a guiding force? Is it the media, which throws truth and objectivity out the window in exchange for promoting its own liberal agenda? Or is it the judiciary, which has single-handedly rewritten our constitution to the point of overturning the very principles upon which this country was founded? The answers are No, No, No, and No.

There is one group and one group alone who is solely responsible for the shame in which we find ourselves.

It is the righteous right. Why do I identify this group as the righteous right? Ecclesiastes 10:2 proclaims that the heart of the fool inclines to the left and the heart of the wise inclines to the right. The Bible identifies the side of right as the righteous side. The Lord promises to uphold us in His righteous right hand (Isa. 41:10). Nothing in the Bible is by chance or without meaning. God could have just as easily identified a righteous left or even more easily not identified a side at all. The mere fact that a side is identified is significant. While the right side is biblically identified with righteousness, the left has historically been defined as sinister, from the Latin root word *sinister*, which means "on the left side."

Even more significant is that throughout history a spiritual war between good and evil, right and wrong, has been waged. I do not believe, therefore, it is coincidence that within our present-day society the moral majority is identified as the extreme, fanatical religious *right*, while the licentious liberals are identified with the *left*. It has always been so. Apparently, even in the days of King Solomon (Eccles. 10:2).

Why is this identification important? To be effective in a battle, it is crucial that you not only are able to identify the enemy, but also are able to identify yourself. The church in America has been so lulled into a state of apathy and deception that it has been unable to do either. How many times have we heard pastors and men of God tell us it is not about party politics?

These occasions are probably too numerous to count. Well, it is time for this error to be denounced. We are fighting a culture war, and I have news for all the pastors and church members who have refused to get down and dirty in the trenches: The battle lines are drawn along party lines. I am not saying nor even intimating that Democrats are not good people or even that they may not be Christians, and I am certainly not saying all Republicans are even remotely Christian. However, what I *am* saying clearly and unequivocally is that you cannot be a Christian who believes in the Bible as the inerrant Word of God and support the Democratic Party's platform either directly or indirectly through its candidates. It is simply impossible, for the simple reason that it is impossible to serve two masters (Matt. 6:24).

The big lie currently promulgated by the media is that while Republicans have the corner on the market of family and morality issues, the Democrats have the corner on the market of benevolence and welfare issues. Such a misperception is infiltrating evangelical youth disenchanted with the right. However, the Democratic position on welfare and benevolence does not align itself with a biblical worldview. One key problem is that most youth today have such a deficient grasp of the Word of God that they fail to see the error in having the federal government play an active role in benevolence.

When I first began practicing law, my mother gave me some very insightful advice. She detailed to me the importance of assessing the strength of my case by watching my opponent. "Honey," she explained, "if your opponents have the facts, they'll argue the facts; if they have the law, they'll argue the law; and if they don't have anything... they'll yell and scream a lot." That advice has served me well on many occasions in the courtroom, and one thing I have noticed on the political front is that the Democratic Party, as a whole, seems to be long on screaming and short on the facts and the law. Let me show you some of the platform distinctions for comparison.

> Because <u>we believe in the</u> privacy and equality of women, we stand proudly for a <u>woman's right to choose</u>, consistent with Roe v. Wade, and regardless of her ability to pay. We stand firmly against Republican efforts to undermine that right. **Democratic Platform**[8] **(emphasis added)**

> We must keep our pledge to the first guarantee of the Declaration of Independence. That is why we say the unborn child has a fundamental individual right to life, which cannot be infringed. We support a human life amendment to the Constitution and we endorse legislation to make it clear that the 14th Amendment's protections apply to unborn children. Our purpose is to have legislative and judicial protection of that right against those who perform abortions. We oppose

using public revenues for abortion and will not fund organizations which advocate it. <u>We support the</u> appointment of judges who respect traditional family values and the <u>sanctity of innocent human life</u>. **Republican Platform**[9] **(emphasis added)**

<u>We support full inclusion of gay and lesbian families in the life of our nation</u> and seek equal responsibilities, benefits, and protections for these families. **Democratic Platform (emphasis added)**

We strongly support a Constitutional amendment that fully protects marriage, and we [oppose] forcing states to recognize other living arrangements as equivalent to marriage. The well-being of children is best accomplished [when] nurtured by their mother & father anchored by the bonds of marriage. <u>We believe that legal recognition and the accompanying benefits afforded couples should be preserved for that unique and special union of one man and one woman which has historically been called marriage.</u> After more than two centuries of American jurisprudence, and millennia of human experience, a few judges and local authorities are presuming to change the most fundamental institution of civilization, the union of a man and a woman in marriage. Attempts to redefine marriage in a single state or city could have serious consequences. **Republican Platform (emphasis added)**

I am pointing out these distinctions so that you will ask yourself which platform seems to be driven by a humanistic worldview, and which one seems to be driven by a biblical worldview? Scripture is clear that abortion is the taking of a life and anyone guilty of such a crime is to fall under the law of *lex talionis*, an eye for an eye or a life for a life (Exod. 21:22-25). Additionally, Scripture makes clear the sanctity of the covenant of marriage and makes equally clear that homosexuality is an abomination the Lord detests (Lev. 18:22, 20:13, Rom. 1:27).

According to Scripture, same-sex relationships are sinful and, like all sin, shameful. Moreover, they are a sign of our crumbling national morality, and same-sex marriages have further undermined the sanctity of marriage and the family. However, by making this assessment, I am by no means intending for us to be cruel and insensitive to those who are walking in such bondage. I do not believe the Lord would desire for us to disregard or fail to witness to those blinded by deceptions. Such deceptions lead to life-draining choices that in turn lead to disease, physical death, and ultimate spiritual death. Yet many times we walk right by those in need, offering no hand of help, or worse yet, giving condemnation without hope.

We are really looking at two very distinct issues. The first issue is our heart of compassion for the lost, which is completely separate from our implementation of proper standards through civil authority. From a biblical standpoint, our endorsement of either party by alignment is a clear signal to society that we abide by the party's platform. I am not saying all Republicans or the Republican Party for that matter are holy and righteous. What I am saying is the Democratic Party platform includes some principles blatantly contrary to the Word of God, and a Christian is not afforded the prerogative of separating their political convictions from personal beliefs. As Jesus said, "No man can serve two masters" (Matt. 6:24).

I am confident these words will greatly offend and even enrage a large percentage of those who read them. However, the reality of the offense lies not with the messenger but with the message, and it is not my message. We all make choices on a daily basis. God tells us clearly we must choose whom we will serve (Josh. 24:15, Deut. 30:19). The shame in which our nation lies today is because too many of those who should be the Righteous Right have chosen comfort or apathy over the scriptural mandate for societal involvement. We are called to be the standard, yet we say and do nothing. God has never needed a majority. All He has ever used was a faithful few to bring deliverance and righteousness.

The shame lies in the fact that Scripture clearly tells us that when the righteous are in power the people will rejoice. I no longer believe this refers solely to those who hold office. Righteous people hold office and get elected only when and where righteous people sway society as a whole. Righteousness exalts a nation (Prov. 14:34). When the Righteous Right holds the keys of control over the direction of a nation, prosperity and hope abound. When the Righteous Right abdicates this responsibility of establishing social standards—well, the fruit we see around us today is exactly what happens.

Who is to blame? I am to blame, because I know the truth and I have not spoken out sooner and louder. If you are a Christian, redeemed by the blood of the Lamb, you are to blame. God did not place us on Earth simply to allow us the opportunity to make our lives orderly and prosperous; He told us to occupy. He told us to take the gospel to and make disciples of all nations (Matt. 28:19). Why did He say *nations* instead of *peoples* of all nations? God called us to the nations because *nations* entail everything: the people, the governments, and the societies as a whole.

Our Founding Fathers recognized that the general principles of Christianity would allow for an unprecedented government—quite literally, a new world. Likewise, God has called Christians to continue to be world-changers, and sadly, American Christians have failed Him at nearly every turn. We are paying a heavy cost for our disobedience when the choice is clear. We must not ever forget Scripture tells us that the heart of the fool inclines to the left, but the heart of the wise inclines to the right (Eccles. 10:2). We are left then with two questions. First, with Scripture decidedly on our side, why then has the Righteous Right abdicated its role within society? And perhaps more importantly, when will we once again occupy our mandated role?

It is painfully obvious that without vision, knowledge, and understanding our nation will perish (Hos. 4:6). We as a nation and as a people must reclaim the Founders' God-given vision for our nation. However, we cannot figure out where we are going until we learn from whence we came. Our heritage provides the most powerful tool of direction for our future. Ours is a heritage rich with purpose and ideals. It is far past time for us to reclaim our heritage, and thereby, our nation.

Chapter Four

THE POWER OF
A HERITAGE

⸻⋙●⋘⸻

HISTORY IS CRUCIAL TO GIVING US DIREC-
tion; even our own personal histories hold
keys to how we should live. Our past has a
way of defining who we are and where we are going.
Scripture tells us it is important for us to reflect on
the past in order to receive direction for the future.
Lamentations 3 is a very bleak chapter at the outset.
The prophet Jeremiah calls to mind all the extreme
trials and difficulties through which he has traveled. It is

important to note that from this reflection upon his past, he comes to a liberating realization for his life, which he begins by saying, "This I recall to mind; therefore I have hope" (v. 21). These memories brought to light the truth of verse 23, that God's mercies are new every morning. As he pondered the hardships of his life, he came to one consistent outcome. Every trial ultimately passed; every sorrow faded into distant obscurity; God's faithfulness always and without fail prevailed. But one thing is certain: Jeremiah could not have seen this pattern but for his willingness to be hind-sighted.

OUR PAST DIRECTS OUR FUTURE

The same is true for nations as well as for individuals. In the Old Testament, God continually calls his people to remember their heritage, especially how they were delivered from Egypt and led to the Promised Land. Deuteronomy 8:2, for example, tells them to "...remember that the Lord your God led you all the way...." In other words, their divinely guided past would give purpose to their present as well as to their future. Deuteronomy 11:2-7 was written at a time when God gave his people commandments by which to live. At this crucial time for God's chosen people, when God was establishing the parameters by which they were to carry out their providence, He begins by reminding them of their rich history, a history overflowing with occurrences that evidenced the greatness of God. From this perspective the Lord detailed how they were to not only remember but also pass on these truths to future generations in order to ensure they stayed the course.

Deuteronomy 11:8 then instructs them, and us, to "[t]each [your] children: When you sit in your house...When you walk by the way...When you lie down...When you rise up." Breaking this down, it basically instructs us to teach the past at all times. Why is our past so important that God commands us to constantly remind our posterity? Simply because without this knowledge, we lose sight of not only who we were but also, more importantly, who we are and where God intends us to go.

Hosea 4:6 tells us, "My people perish for lack of knowledge." A more accurate statement was never made concerning the modern church of the United States of America. Who are we as Americans? In order for us to truly comprehend who we are and who we are intended to be, we must look into our own past.

HISTORICAL TRUTHS

In the early 1400s, there lived a sailor who, while on a voyage to Algeria, encountered a missionary who had been witnessing to the Muslims. This missionary had been stoned and left for dead. The sailor recognized the man to be a well-known evangelist. He carried the man to his ship in hopes of returning him to his homeland. When the ship came within sight of the shores of the missionary's home, they brought him up on deck to see it before he died. The dying missionary instead looked out over the horizon beyond the other side of the ship and proclaimed prophetically, "Beyond this sea, which washes this continent we know, there lies another continent, which we have never seen, whose natives are wholly ignorant of the gospel. Send men there."[10]

With that, the missionary died. The sailor then did what was mandated in Deuteronomy 11:18; he repeated this story to his son and then to his son's son. By this he imparted to his grandson a divine sense of purpose. Who was this grandson? It was none other than Christopher Columbus.

Columbus' famous expedition was birthed in him by a divine call that had been placed on his life as a young boy and was the result of the history passed down to him from his grandfather. Knowing who we are and where we have been are crucial to understanding where it is we are going. This story makes it understandable why Christopher Columbus, in referring to America in a letter to the Queen of Spain in November 1492, stated, "... this was the end and the beginning of the enterprise, that it should be for the enhancement and glory of the Christian religion...."[11]

The fact that the founding of our nation was evangelistic in nature has been repeatedly documented. The

Pilgrims, for example, in the charter document titled the Mayflower Compact, made explicit their intents and purposes in journeying to the New World, declaring, "Having undertaken for the glory of God and advancement of the Christian faith...a voyage to plant the first colony...."[12] This is undeniably our past, and it clearly delineates us as a nation intended to be emphatically Christian.

PASSING ON THE TORCH

If you learn nothing else from this book, please learn this. Truth is not dependent upon majority consent. Truth is truth even if no one accepts it as such. We as a nation were intended by God to be a light set on a hill to serve as a beacon of hope and Christian charity to a lost and dying world. Our history confirms this to be true and its truth is not dependent upon being politically correct. Our Christian past means that, in order for the liberal agenda to succeed, they must first rewrite our nation's history. It is for this reason that liberals find it imperative to alienate us from our past. Their rationale is simple; without knowledge of our heritage, we lose sight of the goals to which we are to be attaining. I perceive this to be the motivating force behind the Democratic Party's need to promote public education to the exclusion of all others. You see, as long as there is freedom in education through private/parochial and home schools, historical teaching cannot be entirely censored. As long as there exists some form of school choice, teaching our Christian heritage, and thus our Christian purpose, cannot entirely be obliterated. I perceive that the liberal agenda of promoting public education to the exclusion of all others is truly just pretext for their control and ability to erase any knowledge of our rich historical past, as well as their desire to conduct social engineering of the minds of all students.

The importance of training our children is second to none. In addition to being a biblical mandate,[13] the greatest thinkers and leaders in our world have recognized that a society's educational values dictate the future of that society. It has been said that the philosophy of the classroom in one generation will be the philosophy of the government in the next.[14] We are currently reaping the socialistic, secularist, humanistic mindset that was propagated within the public-school classrooms of our last generation.

The need to prepare the next generation for the passing of the torch was well understood at one time. Today, such importance seems only to be comprehended within the realm of those who are enemies to the Cross. Why do you think there is such a push within our elementary schools for acceptance of publications that promote tolerance of same-sex relationships? The liberals, unlike us, are keenly aware of the lasting effects of training at a very young age.

Let us take a look at a particular issue to help highlight the effects of training and enlightenment. Were our students allowed to be taught of the historic disapprobation for the practice of sodomy from the age of Christopher Columbus to George Washington forward, they would better understand and appreciate the framework for anti-sodomy laws.

Michele de Cuneo was a young Italian accompanying Christopher Columbus on his voyage in 1495. During this voyage they encountered a very cruel, savage and cannibalistic society known as the Caribs. It became clear that these inhabitants were not only uncivilized cannibals, they were also sodomites to which conduct Cuneo referred as an "accursed vice." He articulated that part of the danger with such behavior was its propensity to spread from society to society.

> "We have judged that this accursed vice may have come to the Indians from those Caribs; because these, as I said before, are wilder men and when conquering and eating those Indians, for spite they may also have committeed that extreme offence, which proceeding thence may have been transmitted from one to the other."[15]

In addition to the concerns for the unsanctioned practice of sexual perversion causing its rapid dissemination, there was the additional concern for the demoralization within our troops. There is a recorded court marshalling of a Lieutenant on March 10, 1778 for the charge of attempting to commit sodomy with another soldier to which such offense George Washington responded as follows.

> "His Excellency the Commander in Chief approves the sentence and with Abhorrence and Detestation of such Infamous Crimes order Liett. Enslin to be drummed out of Camp tomorrow morning by all the Drummers and Fifers in the Army never to return..."[16]

Such clear discourse on the proper handling of the unhealthy practice of sodomy, I would venture to guess, will at no time find its way into the classrooms. Obviously, had there ever been such appreciation for our heritage, rulings such as Lawrence v Allen by our Supreme Court could not have been foisted upon society with the acceptance of being constitutional. This example alone should give us pause as to the enormous impact education may have upon the direction of a society.

During our country's early years, education was viewed as a vehicle to equip students to carry out the Great Commission. The great minds of our young nation were educated at institutions whose creeds, mottoes, and purposes were emphatically Christian. "Cursed be

all that learning that is contrary to the cross of Christ";
"For Christ and the Church"; "To plant, and under the
Divine blessing to propagate in this Wilderness, the
blessed Reformed, Protestant Religion, in the purity of
its Order, and Worship"—these are not statements from
remote and unrenowned Christian institutions. Rather,
these statements come from Princeton, Harvard, and
Yale, respectively.

These statements, when compared to what the
modern-day institutions have become, should serve
to underscore how easily one can deviate from vision
when allowed to forget his or her past. Likewise, it is
frightening to see how far our nation has erred from
our prescribed path. Left unchecked, this distortion will
only increase until we find ourselves in a society wholly
unrecognizable to men of conscience and conviction.
The only safe remedy comes from an accurate perception of our past as found within our charter documents. The intentions of our Founding Fathers were
and are ascertainable, and they are nothing like what is
being propounded by our media, our schools, and our
courts.

We have both truth and the facts on our side. The
crucial question remains whether or not we have the
commitment to fight. I assume if you're reading this
book, the answer is yes, so the next step is to equip you
to fight. If you are truly willing to enter the fray, you
must be appropriately armed, and the first tool in this

warfare is knowledge. Knowledge and understanding are our truest line of defense in this culture war of ideals. To dispel the myths and restore our true heritage, we must be adequately informed. We must begin with how our founding fathers viewed the purpose of civil government within society.

Sir William Blackstone's perception of governments and rightful jurisdiction were drawn directly from the Holy Scriptures. His views were blatant and unequivocal. To understand the mindset of our Founders in drafting our charter documents, one need look no further than to read the boldness in Blackstone's assertion that "[t]his law of nature, being co-eval with mankind and *dictated by God himself,* is of course superior in obligation to any other. It is binding over all the globe, in all countries, and at all times: no human laws are of any validity, if contrary to this; and such of them as are valid derive all their force, and all their authority, mediately or immediately, from this original" (emphasis added). One of my law professors summed up Blackstone like this: "Law is not law if it is contrary to the Laws of Nature and of Nature's God."[17] This is a very meaningful statement and one that will require further review later in this book. It is vitally important to view such a belief as the backdrop for all law at the time of the enactment of our Constitution.

With this belief as a cornerstone, the drafters of our Declaration of Independence and Constitution had to pass all the parameters of civil authority through the litmus test of Holy Scripture. Jurisdiction or the rightful authority of any person, position, or government was carefully crafted so as to comply with the biblical parameters intended for such. Any action or power exercised outside these parameters was viewed as tyrannical. It is, therefore, vitally important for us to possess a clear understanding of proper jurisdiction in order to ascertain legitimate authority. In the next chapter, we will see how the philosophy and writings of such men as Sir William Blackstone influenced the Founders' understanding of civil authority.

Chapter Five

JURISDICTION AND RIGHTFUL AUTHORITY

—————⇒➤●◄⇐—————

THERE IS A SIGNIFICANT DISTINCTION between power and authority. We as a nation have come to accept and equate the fact that our government has the power to control certain aspects of our lives, that it also has the authority to do so. That is not necessarily true and we must know where to draw the line.

JURISDICTION DEFINED

Jurisdiction, simply defined, is the right or authority to govern within a given sphere. Jurisdiction identifies the limits within which one may rightly exercise control. It differs from power in that while one may possess the force or ability to exert control over a particular domain, without rightful authority there is no true jurisdiction. Some of the most egregious infringements upon our freedoms have arisen from the expansion of our governing bodies into areas beyond their proper jurisdiction. More and more areas of our everyday life are annexed into the sphere of governmental control, review, and scrutiny. The broad-sweeping pen of a recent Administration that acquired untold acres of land for National Parks was a vivid and tangible example of private property rights being swallowed up by the gluttonous appetite of a government out of its constraints. When powers are exerted over areas that were never intended to be under the government's control, it makes for a life full of usurped liberties. Unfortunately, American citizens have come to accept that the exercise of power by governmental entities equates to rightful authority; it does not.

Our Founding Fathers were keenly aware of the difference between power and authority. Having so recently witnessed the tyranny birthed from the wrongful exertion of might, they were determined to have the government of their new nation exercise civil authority only within the spheres of proper influence. Hence they created a government of *enumerated* powers only. That is, any power that was not expressly included within the framework of the Constitution was, in fact, expressly excluded. The Tenth Amendment underscored this intent: "The powers not delegated to the United States by the Constitution, nor prohibited by it to the States, are reserved to the States respectively, or to the people." I find this to be significant that the framers placed this as the final article of the Bill of Rights, knowing full well it would be the last words the people would read prior to determining their position on ratification of the Constitution as a whole. I can't help wondering what a difference we would see if our federal government truly operated under this principle today. If we could once again have a Supreme Court that understands this principle, we could make great strides in regaining our liberties.

JURISDICTION UNDERSTOOD

As noted earlier, the major legal treatise that served as the basis for instruction in civil authority at the time of our country's inception was Blackstone's *Commentaries on the Laws of England.* These commentaries were a compilation of laws and principles more popularly referred to as the Common Law. The principles detailed by Blackstone were widely accepted and understood during the crucial years when our country's charter documents were being drafted. To review Blackstone's *Commentaries* is to come to share with the Founders an understanding that our great United States of America was founded by men with a biblical worldview. Such an understanding explains why George Washington proclaimed that the success of our form of government was wholly dependent upon its citizens maintaining that piety and religious conviction as such are the foundation of national morality. "Of all the dispositions and habits which lead to political prosperity," he said in his farewell address, "religion and morality are indispensable supports...[the] firmest props of the duties of Men and citizens." He further was convicted that morality maintained outside of religious conviction was at best a tenuous proposition: "And let us with caution indulge the supposition, that morality can be maintained without religion. Whatever may be conceded to the influence of refined education on minds of peculiar structure, reason and experience both forbid us to expect that national morality can prevail in exclusion of religious principle." How could he have foreseen this almost two centuries prior to the time when we would begin to see the unraveling of our great Republic? He held this insight because he knew the Holy Bible was the source of authority for all the underlying principles of this new land. If a people no longer acknowledged the authority of the Supreme Creator of the Universe, then all the legal parameters espoused by men would be rendered useless. Washington concluded, "No people can be bound to acknowledge and adore the Invisible Hand which conducts the affairs of men more than the people of the United States.... We ought to be no less persuaded that the propitious smiles of Heaven can never by expected on a nation that disregards the eternal rules of order and right which Heaven itself has ordained."

This, unfortunately, is the state in which we as Americans find ourselves today, where the majority "disregards the eternal rules of order and right which Heaven itself has ordained." Blackstone clearly stated, "Law is not law if it is contrary to the laws of Nature and of Nature's God."[18] It was from this biblical litmus test that the parameters for civil government emerged. The Founding Fathers believed this principle and that belief led them to plan a civil government that would govern the people in the most efficacious manner.

Scripture is replete with directives concerning the proper delegation of authority within society. From these commands, we may isolate four areas of identifiable social authority: *civil, ecclesiastical, familial,* and *personal.* Each of these four areas has well-defined lines of jurisdiction with no overlap, so as to not allow for any confusion concerning the purpose and function of each realm of influence. The following paragraphs explore each realm of authority, working outward from the personal to the civil.

Before we go on, however, we must admit a fifth realm of authority: the area of *heart jurisdiction*. This falls within the broad realm of the Heavenly Father's jurisdiction, as the area of each man's heart is exclusively within the Lord's jurisdiction. As the Lord explained to the prophet Samuel, "The Lord does not look at the things man looks at. Man looks at the outward appearance, but the Lord looks at the heart" (1 Sam. 16:7). Scripture further shows us that God alone searches and knows our hearts (Acts 15:8, Rev. 2:23). Therefore, it is not for any man but only the Father above to judge another man's heart.

This must not be confused with the fact that we are called to judge others by their fruit. Matthew 7:16 and 20 enumerate a sort of call to discernment, and this exercise falls within the realm of personal jurisdiction. Personal jurisdiction is the area of personal responsibility, where individuals have authority to make decisions that affect them personally. One of the most definitive commands concerning personal jurisdiction can be found in Micah 6:8. "And what does the Lord require of you? To act justly and to love mercy and to walk humbly with your God."

Familial jurisdiction is the sphere of influence or realm of control we possess within our families. These mutual responsibilities and benefits serve to bring the family into harmony and productivity. This jurisdiction includes areas the Lord has established for spouses toward each other and parents toward children, enabling them to walk in accountability concerning each other. The Scriptures define authority within the confines of marriage and parenting.[19] It tells the wife to submit, the husband to love, the children to obey, and the Fathers to not exasperate the children. Familial jurisdiction also involves areas where the Lord holds parents responsible concerning their children. Examples of this type of jurisdiction include provision. Provision for our households is the family's responsibility. The apostle Paul explains it this way: "If anyone does not provide for his relatives, and especially for his immediate family, he is worse than an unbeliever" (1 Tim. 5:8). Discipline is another example of an area within the jurisdiction of the family. As Hebrews 12:7-9 says, "For what son is not disciplined by his father? If you are not disciplined (and everyone undergoes discipline), then you are illegitimate children and not true sons. Moreover, we have all had human fathers who disciplined us and we respected them for it." Finally, education and training of our children is a prime example of a responsibility that clearly falls within the realm of familial jurisdiction. Scripture is filled with verses holding parents accountable for directing their children through instruction. Examples include Proverbs 22:6; Ephesians 6:4; Deuteronomy 4:9, 6:7, 11:19, 32:46; and Psalms 78:3-6.

Ecclesiastical jurisdiction involves those areas of responsibility for which the Lord holds the church responsible. Benevolence, for example, was to be the duty of the church, not the civil government (James 1:27). To grant this area to civil power is to coerce a man through the involuntary use of his tax dollars to show benevolence when in fact he may not desire to do so. The result is a large section of society resentful for the care and support of others for which they had no desire to be responsible.

Then we have the area of civil jurisdiction, more commonly understood as the framework for governments. The parameters for this authority are plain and simple. The purposes of the civil governing authority are to promote good and discourage or punish wrongdoing (Rom. 13:3-5).

It is important to note here that where God establishes an area of jurisdiction, He holds that entity alone responsible for the manner in which their authority is exercised. Therefore, while such authority may be delegated, it may not be assigned. For example, if I asked you to care for my home in my absence and you consented, then you alone bear the authority and responsibility for such care. Should you then decide to hire a security company and/or lawn care service to carry out the task, that would be delegated authority. However, you do not have the legal right to assign or transfer the responsibility for the care such that if something goes amiss, notwithstanding any contractual rights you may have against the security or lawn care companies, you alone are responsible. The same is true with our jurisdictional responsibilities concerning our children. While we may choose to delegate some of our authority to others, such as teachers, we may not assign the ultimate responsibility. As between God and ourselves, we are the only ones He will ultimately hold accountable. Therefore, when the civil government comes in and attempts to declare themselves the ultimate authority on the care and/or education of our children, this is an unlawful usurpation of jurisdiction. God will not hold the state responsible and, consequently, that authority cannot be assigned to the state or civil authorities. Such a belief system stems from the Greek philosophy of *parens patriae*. While this belief was modified under the English Common Law to be a responsibility of the sovereign to care for the disabled, the general view was one of ultimate authority resting in the state as parent. You may view such despotism to be fantasy more than fact, but the frightening truth is much of our American society embraces the belief that the parents are not the ultimate authority. Compulsory education laws, while cloaked within the auspices of legitimacy, have been used to undermine the authority of the parent in deciding what is best for their children. I am in no way advocating ignorance or illiteracy. However, no matter how noble a cause may appear, where it extends beyond the boundaries of its rightful jurisdiction, the potential for tyranny is greatly enhanced.

Now that we have the same understanding of jurisdiction in mind that our Founding Fathers possessed, it is easy to understand why they created the "free exercise" clause and the "no establishment" clause of the First Amendment, and to understand why it was the *First* Amendment. We as citizens of this government were to possess a completely undeniable right to "walk humbly with our God" or, as they put it, to worship God according to the dictates of our conscience. They knew and completely understood that worship fell within the parameters of personal jurisdiction and could in no way be infringed upon by the civil government. As to the no establishment clause, the same can be said, that this area of worship was to be governed by personal jurisdiction alone, and as such the civil government had no authority to interfere with this personal liberty in any fashion. This is a wholly different concept from the widely accepted doctrine of separation of church and state, which is conspicuously absent from the text of the Constitution. It is this fallacious principle, as erroneously applied to our society, which is ultimately responsible for denying the right of children to pray in school. Upon understanding the true intent of our founding Fathers in the no establishment clause, it becomes immediately clear that their intent is not being even remotely served by the wrongful extension of civil power into an area that clearly falls within personal jurisdiction.

This intrusion into our liberties becomes greatly pronounced by the wrongful exertion of civil power into familial jurisdiction by the abdication of parents and the usurpation of government in the area of education. When viewing our society from a biblical worldview, it becomes apparent that the *parens patriae* doctrine of society espoused by the Greeks (and now implemented into our Christian republic) is incompatible with our Constitution. "It takes a village to raise a child" is actually a very old concept. The Greeks held that the government, or the state, was ultimately parent to all children and thus responsible for their upbringing, and this philosophy is being touted again. The problem is that it is a theory inconsistent with the biblical perception our Founding Fathers used in establishing our great nation.

Another example of the confusion that abounds from jurisdictional error is the hate crimes legislation. These laws serve only to do one of two things. Either they are discriminatory laws, and thus contrary to the Fourteenth Amendment by preferring certain victims on the basis of their race or sexual preference, or they are laws that rather than judging people's actions, are judging people's hearts, an area reserved strictly for the Lord. The end result is that they make no sense and cause a great deal of harm. Whatever happened to *lex talionis,* the "eye for an eye and life for a life" rationale that actually makes sense?

On the contrary, I fail to see how any act of murder is anything other than a hate crime. How can it be otherwise when Scripture tells us that to hate is like committing murder in our hearts (Matt. 5:21)? I would like to see any one of the state or federal legislators who voted for these indefensible laws explain to a parent why the murderer of their precious baby girl or boy is not guilty of a hate crime. How can they justify valuing the life of another victim more highly, simply because he is in a class of "favored victims" and, consequently, his assailant is inequitably subject to a greater punishment? That is offensive to anyone who has lost a loved one who did not fit within the protected categories.

How has this legislation been able to stand up to constitutional scrutiny? After all, it is a direct violation of the Fourteenth Amendment that says, "No state shall deny to any person within its jurisdiction the equal protection of the laws." Clearly, victims are not equally protected under these laws if a victim's assailant faces harsher punishment solely on the basis of the victim's identity. The only other option is that the government has now elected to judge the heart and its motives rather than merely the actions of the person. If this is the case, then these laws create a very frightening usurpation of jurisdiction that opens the door to serious governmental intrusions.

It does not take long to see that a few of these jurisdictional errors make for a great deal of mayhem within our society. Unless and until the citizens of our great nation begin to realize rightful authority, and thus reject wrongful assertion of power, we will be unable to find solutions to many of our social and political dilemmas. Once we understand the biblical worldview accepted by our Founding Fathers, we must begin to elect officials committed to that worldview. If we do not, we must prepare ourselves for the inevitable erosion of our republican form of government. This erosion, unchecked, will produce a country wholly unrecognizable as the "land of the free, and the home of the brave."

Why are there no ramifications for when our governing authorities run amok? Why is it that the bulk of society has silently acquiesced to this blatant erosion of our precious blood-bought liberties? Why is there no corporate voice crying out for accountability to keep those in power in check? The answer saddens me. The very voice that made our country great at its inception is now silent as the grave.

The church in America was once an outspoken proponent of liberty, freedom, and independence. As difficult as it is to accept, it is the silence of the church in America that has allowed our greatest shame. Even more difficult to accept is a central reason for our silence. As the next chapter will show, it appears that too many churches have switched their allegiance from

God and Country to Money and Prosperity, with tragic consequences.

Chapter Six

SILENCING
THE LAMBS

———⟫●⟪———

A MODERN-DAY HOLOCAUST HAS BEEN
allowed to go unchecked for too long because
of the silence of the church. Untold millions
of innocent lives have been lost while the church has
watched quietly on the sidelines. "True religion" unde-
filed includes speaking out for the orphans or the father-
less, says the book of James (1:22). A society that fails to
recognize the sanctity of human life is a society on the
brink of collapse. Still, countless precious babies have

been led to the slaughter day after day while the church refuses to get in the fray. The church has a biblical obligation to speak out and protect the defenseless. Why then have American Christians remained silent? To find part of the answer, we must look to an unlikely place: the United States Tax Code.

THE TRUE IMPACT OF THE 501(C)3 AT WORK

The federal budget of 1993 included the largest tax increase in our nation's history and brought taxation levels to an all-time high. This factor alone was probably responsible for the sweeping victory of Republican candidates in 1994, ushering in the first Republican majority in Congress in over forty years. It has been estimated that the resultant burden placed upon hardworking, middle-class Americans forced them to work until May before they are able to net any true profits for their families for any given year. Tax credits and exemptions were being sought at a premium, which highlighted a much more serious concern: an all-pervasive desire to avoid taxation at all costs.

The sad truth is, however, that such a desire existed even prior to this additional tax burden, and it continues to exist within our society. This stealthy idea has increasingly woven its web until it has created a stranglehold on our freedom of speech. The consuming desire to obtain tax-exempt status has given rise to the greatest denial of this First Amendment protection since the inception of our great nation.

One need not look very closely at American history to discover that American pastors were in large part responsible for the growing consensus of our need for independence from Great Britain. It was their heart-felt convictions, delivered with a burning fervor that sparked the flame of freedom in the hearts of their parishioners. Many of them spoke out in direct defiance of the ramifications they could have suffered at the hands of Loyalists and the King's governing authorities. But for these brave patriots, their convictions outshone their fears. Unfortunately, in today's society, shepherds of such passion and conviction are difficult to find. While the silencing factor is no longer fear of imprisonment or death, it appears to be more persuasive in its ability to keep the church in America from speaking out. What method now in force gags the church? It is simply the desire to be and to remain tax-exempt.

Almost without fail, one of the first orders of business for institutions possessing a biblical worldview is to acquire the coveted designation of 501(c)3. The name derives from the section of the tax code that provides tax exemption to certain non-profit organizations. Due to the government's inappropriate stance that it shall tax every entity unless such entity makes certain concessions to its control, it appears that such concessions have become the accepted norm within the parameters of religious institutions. The truth of the matter is that our Founding Fathers believed religion or "the duties we owed to God" to be preeminent to the control of the civil state. This quote comes from James Madison, commonly called the Father of our Constitution because of the extensive contributions he made to the Supreme Law of our Land. However, the fact that our civil government frequently and inappropriately infringes upon our civil liberties should in no way coerce us into responses which are contrary to biblical mandates.

I recently had a discussion with a gentleman who works with a charitable organization. This particular organization's vision and ideals I wholeheartedly support. The distressing part of our discussion centered on the limitations and infringements upon the organization's ability to speak out on issues about which the organization was profoundly concerned. His comment was one that is far too often expressed by the church. It is a belief that has become firmly rooted in our belief systems, and it is a lie straight from the pit of Hell: that the church can neither speak out openly on matters of politics and public affairs nor take sides. This erroneous perception is further underscored by a supplemental deception that the church must be a 501(c)3 entity and, therefore, must yield its freedom to speak out concerning certain issues. Those who believe this lie are either ignorant of the truth or have used it as a cloak to cower behind in order to not have to address those topics most controversial in society.

Our civil government's current misperception that they possess any rights whatsoever to tax the corporate body of Christ is irrelevant to this most crucial issue of the heart. Where do our responsibilities lie as the church of Jesus Christ? Are they to God or mammon? We cannot answer, "Both," or the truth is not in us, for Jesus himself has said we cannot serve two masters. When the body of Christ is faced with the choice of paying taxes or rendering total allegiance to our King, we have overwhelmingly chosen mammon. When Christ himself was asked about the arguably over-burdensome and inappropriate taxes of Caesar, He did not take the time to address or excuse compliance on the basis of inappropriate civil authority. Instead, He went straight to the heart of the matter, "...render unto Caesar that which is Caesar's and unto God that which is God's" (Matt. 22:21).[20] The only time we are under a biblical mandate of civil disobedience is when obeying the law impedes our allegiance to God. Our government's erroneous taxation position is in no way preventing the church from boldly speaking out, as God requires, for we are still left with a choice. Our choice is much easier than that of the early church martyrs, who likewise had a choice either to disobey God in order to save their earthly lives or to obey God by speaking out and thereby face flogging, imprisonment, or even martyrdom. What a wimpy, disobedient body we have become when, faced with the choice of disobeying God in order not to pay taxes or obeying God and paying the taxes (Rom. 13:7), we choose to allow the civil government to buy our silence.

Perhaps a quick lesson in history at this time would be helpful. Most people know Patrick Henry is famous for his quote "Give me liberty or give me death." Very few people are aware of the events that originally inspired this speech. When Patrick Henry was a young attorney, he rode into the town of Culpeper, Virginia, only to encounter a man beaten and in the stocks. Young Mr. Henry inquired as to this man's crime and was informed that the man was a minister who refused to be licensed by the state. Such a requirement was basically a means for Great Britain to dictate what was acceptable and what was unacceptable material on which to preach. The minister refused to let anyone, other than God, dictate the content of his sermons and as a result was beaten and publicly humiliated. Not much later, the minister was again beaten, this time so seriously that he died from his wounds. This example makes it clear to whom that minister gave his allegiance. Sadly, the example of the modern church makes it equally obvious to whom we owe our allegiance as well.

It is time for the church to be heard as a powerful voice of truth and mercy in our society once again. We must dispel the myth that the church "cannot speak out" and refuse to accept that as an excuse anymore. I realize many churches and pastors who read this will be greatly offended. It must be so since Christ has said He is an offense to all, and because Christ is the Word, His Word must be a source of offense. However, it is my prayer that there is a remnant of pastors out there who are passionate about the truth and desire to make their voices heard. I fervently hope and believe this information may be the key to liberating them, that they will not be silenced, and theirs will become voices in the wilderness, crying out, "Repent, for the Kingdom of God is at hand!"

It is for these few brave visionaries I write these words. I know God has raised you up for such a time as this. It would take courage to stand up and tell your congregation that if faced with the choice between remaining a tax-exempt entity and the freedom to speak out unfettered, that you would choose to render to Caesar that which is Caesar's and unto God that which is God's. God is and will be your source, not your 501(c)3 status, and He will continue to abundantly provide as you are obedient to His Word. It is urgent that your voice be heard because the church in America is like a flock of sheep scattered without a shepherd. We are a lost and bewildered people who are desperately in need of spiritual guidance. Will you be one of God's elect to pick up the staff and lead us as a nation into heartfelt repentance? The choice is yours. Choose you this day whom you will serve.

This willingness to speak out on the issues may seem rather benign. However, it is when the Chrstian community stays silent that moral relativism and ultimate decay remain unchecked. From the abomination of enslaving an entire group of people, to the atrocities of the holocaust to the present-day slaughter of innocent life, the consequences of keeping silent are devastating.

Chapter Seven

SLAVE, JEW, AND BABY, TOO

——————⇒⊙⇐——————

S INCE THE DAWN OF TIME, MAN HAS SOUGHT
to find some superiority in himself that he could
in turn lord over others. It is an age-old barbarism that finds its way into almost every society. The
extent of its acceptance is generally contingent upon
the moral state of the citizens within a given society.
Slavery within these United States was nothing less
than the denial of the sanctity of human life. The slaveholders were not solely to blame, for had not the general

tenor of society been at least tolerable of this uncivilized and barbaric treatment of human beings, the practice could not have continued for the length of time it did. Who then was to blame for slavery? In short, those who opposed slavery but said or did nothing to aid in its abatement were as much to blame as were those who did not oppose it, as well as those who demanded its unfettered continuance.

The Denial of Human Rights

Few issues ever become as heatedly contested or controversial as those issues that should be obvious to every civilized human being. Slavery, for example, was the source of numerous altercations that echoed even within the halls of our assumedly dignified Capitol. For only one example, consider the confrontation between future president James K. Polk and Congressman (and former president) John Quincy Adams.

Modern historians, in their attempt to rewrite history, will rarely, if ever, tell the unbiased truth. Liberal elitists within our society have rewritten history so that one would only know James K. Polk to be a noble man of tremendous vision whose leadership occasioned the broad expansion of our great frontier. A loyal Democrat will never have you know the other side of James K. Polk. Polk was the Speaker of the House when the call for impeachment of Congressman, and former President,

John Quincy Adams was made. A Tennessean, Polk was typical of the Southern Democrats of his day, a devout defender of slaveholders' rights. To argue for the rights of slaves was grounds to demand that a Southern gentleman be given the right to defend his honor in a duel.

The outcry to impeach Massachusetts congressman John Quincy Adams was aroused simply upon the grounds that he had allegedly called for the House to entertain a writ of petition from a group of slaves. The House floor was in an outrage and wanted their pound of flesh exacted from this man for daring to attribute any rights to this group of slaves, who were to be viewed as possessing no rights. The Southern Democratic Representatives, which group included Polk, needed to silence any effort viewed as a threat to their rights to own slaves. Despite Polk's efforts, Adams was not impeached.[2]

The fact remains that none of the atrocities perpetrated against slaves could have ever taken place had there not been an accepted diminution of the sanctity of human life. The slaveholders and those defending them had successfully convinced the bulk of society there was nothing inherently wrong in their conduct as, after all, blacks did not possess the same human worth as did whites. On this side of the controversy, the heinousness of this belief is appalling. The moral conscience of our society has since been awakened to see that no greater worth exists in any particular human being that in any way should be exerted as superior over the rights of another. You would think then that as societies progress such backward beliefs could not in any way dare to raise their evil heads. One can only dream that someday this would become true.

CIVILIZED SOCIETY REMAINS UNCIVILIZED

On the contrary, "enlightened" society has shown itself capable of similar, and even greater, atrocities. The horrors of the Holocaust still cause shockwaves within the hearts and minds of individuals of conscience. There are no words to describe the demonic mindset of those persons who inflicted such evils upon another group of human beings. Indeed, when faced with the reality of the Holocaust, we are left with a single question: How could such a tragedy occur during the enlightened era of the Twentieth Century?

Hitler's success in effectuating his plan required that he first accomplish the task of dehumanizing the Jews. In order to carry out his diabolical regime, it was crucial that he cause a significant proportion of society to accept the position that the Jews were a threat and of less innate human worth than other segments of the population. Again, we see that the most extreme denials of human rights are only occasioned upon a widespread acceptance that certain human beings are by nature inferior to another group of human beings, and as such, have fewer or no rights.

The greatest distress to me in all of these tragedies is not that there exist a few extremist individuals who possess a perverted heir of supremacy that leads them to great evils through their seared consciences. There always has been and always will be evil. What shocks me more are the masses which are in such a declined moral state that they can be lulled into acceptance of what should appear a blatant denial of human rights. Unfortunately, the same premise of supremacy that has been the foundation for numerous assaults on the dignity of humanity never ceases to find new ways to imbed itself into the heart of society.

From the Israeli slaves in Egypt to the Cherokee Trail of Tears, we hear the same old tale unfolding in the lives of a new group of people, namely, that some human beings are labeled of less worth than that of their oppressors. The oppressors attempt to salve their consciences with the lie that their rights are somehow superior to the rights of those they oppress. The argument may also be made that the oppression is somehow a service to society. If this argument does not sound familiar, it should. It is once again being avidly voiced, this time in defense of the barbaric atrocities occasioned in the name of "a woman's right to choose."

SAME GAME, NEW NAME

The average American would be sickened at the thought of scissors being thrust in at the base of a baby's skull as he is being born and then pried apart in order for the brain to be extracted. Perhaps I am deluded, but my faith in the American people makes me believe they have sufficient moral character that they would not want to see this type of a procedure conducted on a dog, much less upon a human infant. There is no group of our society who is more innocent and defenseless than these tiny babies, who cannot even speak for themselves. Yet our society, instead of protecting them and their inalienable right to life, is arbitrarily denying that right on the grounds that a woman possesses a superior right not to be fettered or inconvenienced by the life of another human being. The liberals have added further insult to injury through their support of abortion on demand including partial-birth abortion. Of course, one of the most blatant in his disregard for human life is the Democratic Presidential Nominee, the same person who wants everyone to believe he is a devout Christian.

The arrogant refusal to abide by proper moral parameters to protect innocent life is the same sort of fascist, supremacist attitude exhibited by Mussolini and Hitler. Christians should be grateful that we have had a president with the courage and conviction to sign the ban on partial-birth abortions, as well as for his willingness to fight for the protection of snowflake babies, children born from embryos created by in vitro fertilization. Once a society embraces a quality of life standard over the sanctity of life, no life is sacred.

We must wake up and see the extent of the threat we as human beings face. If we do not maintain a unified front that we will not tolerate or allow the denial of fundamental rights to any human being at the expense of another group of human beings, then we all walk on extremely thin ice. Once we allow any group to successfully postulate its position of supremacy, then every one of us is in danger of becoming part of a new group viewed to be of inferior worth. This could never happen, you may argue. All I have to say in response to such blindness is, "How soon they forget." Look at the Democratic Party, the party whose platform relentlessly advocates the supremacy of a woman's rights over those of her baby. Furthermore, see how the party still courts both blacks and Jews who, by embracing the party, ultimately embrace the position that gave rise to their own oppression. It appears that any and all human beings are capable of dehumanizing another group of human beings, as long as they do not fall into the category of the oppressed at the time the argument is being made.

President Reagan saw the connection between slavery and abortion. He addressed it eloquently and his words bear repeating. He said, "Abraham Lincoln recognized that we could not survive as a free land when some men could decide that others were not fit to be free and should therefore be slaves. Likewise, we cannot survive as a free nation when some men decide that others are not fit to live and should be abandoned to abortion or infanticide. My administration is dedicated to the preservation of America as a free land, and there is no cause more important for preserving that freedom than affirming the transcendent right to life of all human beings, the right without which no other rights have any meaning."[22]

I have felt compelled to champion this issue not only because I believe it is a most telling factor as to the moral state of our nation, but also because I am in a unique position to do so as a woman. Too often, when insightful and compassionate males present the same position on this issue, they are labeled male chauvinist pigs. But this is not a conflict between male and female, nor is it really a conflict between "life" and "choice." In the same way, the real battles were not between abolitionists and slaveholders, or Jews and Nazis. Rather, all these conflicts have to do with right and wrong. It is always right to defend every human being's right to life; it is always wrong to elevate one human being's rights over another's, simply on the basis of some secondary classification. It has always been the case, and it always will be the case, irrespective of any society's general acceptance or denial of this truth.

It further saddens me to consider the number of people who believe that if abortion is sin, then capital punishment must be, too. Or conversely, some believe that if you support capital punishment, then you must support abortion. Even a child playing "One of these things is not like the other..." would be able to see the glaring difference between abortion and capital punishment. Abortion is the senseless taking of innocent life, while capital punishment is the taking of a life as a penalty for wrongdoing.

It is also disheartening to note the number of people who argue that capital punishment is not Christian. Such people clearly do not know the meaning of the word Christian. The word *Christian* means to be a follower of Jesus Christ. This obtains deeper meaning when one acknowledges that Jesus was identified in scripture as the Word of God made flesh. Therefore, to follow Christ is to follow the Word of God. "We know that we have come to know him if we obey his commands. The man who says, 'I know him,' but does not do what he commands is a liar, and the truth is not in him. But if anyone obeys his word, God's love is truly made complete in him. This is how we know we are in him; Whoever claims to live in him must walk as Jesus did." [I John 2:3-6]. Jesus confirmed that He did not come to abolish the Law but to fulfill it. Killing someone is murder and sin, as is harboring hatred in your heart. It is also true that when someone is murdered, the victim's blood cries out from the land for justice (Genesis 4:10).

Furthermore, both the protection of the innocent and the punishment of the guilty are areas that fall squarely within the sphere of civil jurisdiction. Therefore, the disingenuous argument that one may personally oppose abortion but feel it is not an issue for the government is operating on simply that, feelings. Such a person is wholly ignorant of the true function of civil government, and if such a person is in the church, they should be warned they are walking on the shaky ground of being lukewarm. The Scripture is clear that God will spew such a person out of his mouth. We are not allowed as Christians to take middle-of-the-road, politically correct positions. Truth will always be a threat to our hedonistic tendencies and those who desire to proclaim such truth cannot be wimpy, spineless popularity-seekers, tossed to and fro with every wind of change. Instead, we must be willing to stand up and fight on behalf of the defenseless, despite how the world may hate us.

We have an urgent duty as a civilized nation to stop this rampant new holocaust, which has occasioned the slaughter of more innocent lives since its inception than any other trampling of human rights in the history of mankind. Once the pro-abortionists tipped their hand and ceased to make viability the issue but rather the supremacy of women's rights over their babies', we must ask who, then, will be next? If we as an allegedly civilized society can continue to condone the inhumane annihilation of an innocent group of human beings, God help us all.

We must also ask ourselves, how did we get to this deplorable state of barbarism? We need not look far before we realize the first major chink in our armor came from the Supreme Court. How many times have we heard *Roe v. Wade* proclaimed as the law of the land? For over a generation we have accepted this lie that *Roe v. Wade* is law. The big problem with this argument is simply this—courts cannot make law; not even the Supreme Court of the United States has the constitutional authority to make law. It would appear that one of the first areas we as a nation need to address in our battle to reclaim decency is to dispel the lie that the Supreme Court is all-powerful. We must rein in this runaway branch of government, and if we fail to do so, we may loose all of our freedoms without there ever being another attack on our shores.

Chapter Eight

THE CAPRICIOUS
COURT

⸺⸺►●◄⸺⸺

I AM DISMAYED BY THE PREVALENT ACCEPTANCE
of the broadened jurisdiction of judicial authority.
Almost without fail, justification for this unconstitutional expansion of Article III power is based
upon dicta within the landmark decision of *Marbury
v Madison*. An erroneous reading of this decision has
become so routinely accepted that the precedent of
judicial supremacy is never questioned. I find myself in
a position similar to those who first declared the Earth

to be round rather than flat, that is, correct but in the distinct minority. Still, error is error despite its acceptance by the vast majority.

Our republican form of government does not allow for majority rule where it directly conflicts with the rule of law. We are, after all, a government of laws, not of men. We are not a pure democracy, but rather a democratic republic. The bottom line is that our Constitution grants to society great latitude in allowing for input into our representative form of government, but only to the extent that the Constitution is upheld.

Legal scholars present a unified front on their erroneous interpretation of *Marbury v. Madison.* The Constitution explicitly states that it is the supreme law of the land. Consequently, to support the argument that commentary within a case such as *Marbury v. Madison* grants ultimate supremacy to the judiciary over the other two branches is constitutional heresy. I vehemently disagree with this reading of *Marbury* and the resultant judicial legislation. If this were in fact the position of the Court in *Marbury,* such a precedent would make the Constitution's checks upon the judiciary of no effect. The Court did not—nor does it now—possess the authority to amend the Constitution in this fashion. Alexander Hamilton expressed his belief in a strong Constitution in a letter to Senator James A. Bayard of Delaware. "In my opinion," he wrote in April 1802, "the present constitution is the standard to which we are to cling. Under its banner bona fide must we combat our political foes, rejecting all changes but through the channel itself provided for amendments."[23]

If the Founders intended to grant the judiciary the authority to give meaning to all laws, the powers given to the legislature in Article I would in essence be included within the sphere of judicial authority. In other words, there would have been no need for separate articles, and the resulting separation of powers. Such an interpretation of *Marbury* would do what Justice Oliver Wendell Holmes later declared: make the decisions of the Supreme Court the supreme law of the land. Acceptance of this argument rises to the level of Constitutional heresy, as it serves to undermine our constitutional form of government and ignores the fact that the Constitution is a document of enumerated powers. The Founders knew firsthand that power unchecked was the fastest vehicle toward the subjugation of the peoples' rights. Consequently, those powers not included or explicitly assigned to the government or one of its branches were intended to be purposefully excluded. This careful construction of checks and balances upon the separate branches is totally undermined by the modern-day acceptance of the Supreme Court's ability to create law.

Marbury cannot reasonably be interpreted to extend judicial authority to this argued sphere of supremacy. The argument for judicial supremacy is wholly incongruous with the *Marbury* Court's ultimate decision that it *lacked* jurisdiction to decide the case because the Constitution denied the court original jurisdiction over such matters. In other words, case decisions apply to cases or controversies alone and cannot be elevated to the level of law without engulfing legislative authority. To deny this check is to nullify the clear and separate powers of the branches of government as delineated within the Constitution. Alexander Hamilton denounced such a usurpation of power as tyranny, as we will see shortly. Hamilton considered respect for the Constitution "the greatest source of our security in a Republic." In the same letter, written to the *American Daily Advertiser,* he wrote that "A sacred respect for the constitutional law is the vital principle, the sustaining energy of a free government."[24]

Justification is now being crafted to defend the rogue courts of today. I have even heard it argued that President Jefferson's silence concerning *Marbury* was proof of his acceptance of judicial supremacy over the executive branch. This argument is illogical. To start with an erroneous interpretation and argue that silence and inactivity is proof that such an interpretation was indeed commonly accepted does not follow reason. Rather, the President's inactivity was more likely occasioned from two much more plausible reasons. First, there was no need to complain of non-compliance with constitutional checks and balances because the ruling did not in fact proclaim judicial supremacy as is argued. Second, had the Court stepped over the boundaries of their constitutional authority, it was the legislative branch, not the executive, that was vested with the authority to impeach the Supreme Court justices for failing to operate within the bounds of their authority.

In the *Federalist Papers,* Alexander Hamilton detailed how he had no fear of the judicial branch, as it was clearly the weakest branch of all three, not a viewpoint conducive to the arrogance and supremacy exhibited by modern-day courts. Further, Hamilton explained that while the inclusion of legislative authority within the judicial branch would have devastating effects, such tyrannical usurpation of constitutional authority was not viewed as a realistic threat. The reason for this was simple. How, Hamilton reasoned, would the judicial branch ever dare to encroach upon the powers of the legislature when the legislature was the very branch vested with the authority to impeach judges for such actions? You read that correctly: Usurpation of legislative authority is grounds for the legislature to impeach judges, even Supreme Court justices. Therefore, the only reasonable and constitutional interpretation of *Marbury* is that it stands for the premise of well-defined jurisdictional authority with the duty of the Court to simply reiterate the express, enumerated language of the Constitution in relation to a specific case or controversy. In no way did this decision extend or create constitutional law through the vehicle of interpretation, nor could it. In truth, *Marbury* stands for the premise that the Supreme Court must not exercise authority over any area outside the Constitution's delineation, which was then readily accepted as the supreme law of the land. To accept any other interpretation is to provide an internal means by which a single branch of government might surreptitiously override our constitutional form of government without meeting the requisite standards to amend the Constitution. I cannot accept such an interpretation, nor did our Founding Fathers, and nor should any citizen who values the freedoms and liberties that are secured by our great Constitution.

James Madison, commonly referred to as the Father of the Constitution, warned that error steeped in precedent would lead to tyranny. Clearly he was accurate in his assessment. We know all too well that accepting the erroneous interpretation of *Marbury* and allowing it to become steeped in further precedent has opened the door to judicial tyranny. With broad, sweeping acceptance that case decisions establish precedents that rise to the level of tertiary law, how can the error ever be corrected? Today, case decisions are viewed as forming legal precedents and as such have become an excuse for insubordination to constitutional authority.

Chapter Nine

EROSION FROM WITHIN

———⟫●⟪———

EW DOCTRINES HAVE ALLOWED SUCH AN extensive internal attack upon the checks and balances of our governmental branches, as has the doctrine of *stare decisis.* This doctrine of "case precedents" is considered by legal scholars to be necessary for the consistency of court decisions, both from jurisdiction to jurisdiction as well as from lower court to higher court. However, upon closer scrutiny, we may rightly suspect it as less a necessity and more a means of justifying judicial legislation.

Before I embark upon what I hope will be a moment of revelation as concerns the deception of the doctrine of *stare decisis,* I must back up and first explain what role this doctrine is currently said to play. *Stare decisis,* in plain and simple English, means that when a decision or a ruling on a particular matter of law is rendered, that ruling provides more than mere direction for other courts entertaining the same laws. Rather, it establishes a precedent that rises to the level of a law that is to be followed. Consequently, when a court of superior authority renders a decision, the decision is viewed as binding on all lower courts. In other words, lower courts act as if they have no more discretion to veer from these case decisions when dealing with a similar case or controversy than they would from statutory or constitutional law. The only time a case precedent can be avoided is when a court of equal authority or a higher court finds the prior decision to be erroneous and reverses or overturns the previously established case precedent. Such reversals, as you can imagine, are few and far between. Such a decision requires an extensive review of the underlying law as well as second-guessing the prior court's assessment of this law. The courts enjoy neither practice, for it establishes a protocol whereby they themselves may someday be scrutinized.

Now, one might ask, "Well, just exactly what is wrong with consistency in court rulings? Doesn't this constrain rogue judges from entering their decisions on a whim?" There is, of course, nothing wrong with consistency in judicial decision-making. Unfortunately, we Americans have bought the lie that the safeguard of this consistency lies in the hands of *stare decisis*. It does not. Rather, I believe that *stare decisis* was a clever disguise under which our judicial branch of government elevated its powers from being subordinate to those of Congress, as was intended by our Founding Fathers, to being superior to every other branch. Madison saw the tendency for this attitude of supremacy and denounced it saying, "As the courts are generally the last in making the decision, it results to them, by refusing or not refusing to execute a law, to stamp it with its final character. This makes the judiciary... paramount in fact to the legislature, which was never intended, and can never be proper."[25]

Our Constitution is clear about its declaration upon its face to be "the Supreme Law of the Land." However, liberal Supreme Court justices have usurped this supremacy by arguing that their position as the great interpreters of the Constitution in fact makes *them* the highest law. Such a blatant attempt to modify the intents and purposes of our Constitution should be called what it is: an impeachable offense. Instead it is lauded as truth in every courtroom and law school in America.

Why has this been the case? Why have the courts been given a pass on what is clearly beyond the pale? In my opinion, this injustice is evidence of the deeper spiritual battle we are facing. Giving the judiciary carte blanche has allowed this one branch to single-handedly denigrate our Christian heritage within our constitutional form of government. These spiritual battle lines have been drawn in our society, as may be seen by the support of the liberal media who view the courts as their vehicle to alter our republican form of government to conform to their caprice rather than the intents and purposes of our Founding Fathers. I do not believe that the public at large would have agreed to such a usurpation of powers, and so it became necessary to hide behind a doctrine of general acceptance in an effort to successfully effectuate these changes.

Stare decisis has become an unnecessary evil in our judicial branch for the following reasons. First, its only purpose, argued by its supporters, is to foster consistency among court rulings. However, the purpose of the judicial branch is simply to apply existing law to a particular case or controversy. Our Constitution makes it clear that law should only be promulgated by Article I power, not Article III power. Article I defines within the Constitution the powers given to the legislative branch. Article III concerns itself with the powers the Constitution grants to the judicial branch. Consequently, the judiciary's purpose is to simply take a given set of facts in a particular case or controversy and apply either constitutional or statutory law.

What then is the function of the court if no law can be found which applies to a case or controversy before them? Today such a situation is viewed as an opportunity for the courts to read into or extend from the existing laws some applicable meaning and thereby creating new law, or legislating from the bench. Such "law" must then be followed as precedent. This modern function does not comply with the Supreme Court's power as defined by Article III of the Constitution. Rather, the Constitution would mandate that the Courts simply announce they have no jurisdiction to decide the matter as no law is currently in existence addressing such an issue. The Courts were never intended to be a free-for-all venue that addressed every conflict within our society, making up laws along the way. The judiciary was intended only to be a forum where existing laws would be applied to a particular case or controversy. Were it not so, members of the judicial branch would be elevated to the level of lawmakers and yet would not be in the same position of accountability to their constituency as those in the legislative branch, as envisioned by our Founders in the Representative form of government.

How then do we address the consistency of rulings argument so readily accepted in defense of *stare decisis*? The answer is very simple. If our judges are truly held to the constraints of their authority as outlined within the

Constitution, then their task would be to review existing constitutional (primary) or statutory (secondary) law and apply it to the facts before them. If every judge would do that—and only that—the decisions would be just as consistent as they are after researching and following case precedence (which has become known as tertiary law). The fallacy of such a doctrine should be obvious by the mere denomination of a case holding as "law." Why should it lend any more consistency for a court to research all applicable case decisions and apply those decisions, than for a court to research the much less voluminous statutory or constitutional law and apply those laws to the case before the court? The answer is, it doesn't. It is a farce that has been used to provide a vehicle to grow the judiciary's power through judicial fiat.

STARE DECISIS IN ACTION

To see the extent of the damage that has been accomplished through *stare decisis,* we need look no further than the "right of privacy" dicta established by the U.S. Supreme Court in the 1923 case *Meyer v. Nebraska.* This fictional right was later used by the Court as a precedent for expanding interpretation of the Ninth Amendment to legalize abortions in *Roe v. Wade.* The error of *Roe v. Wade*—and, for that matter, *Meyer*—is clear when one remembers, as stated above, that our Constitution is a document of enumerated powers. In short, if a power was not expressly enumerated in the Constitution, then it should be considered purposely excluded.

How then could they expand the Ninth Amendment by their "penumbras of emanations" argument? They did so by hanging their hat on case precedents that the courts and the legislature had allowed to be elevated to the level of constitutional law. These prior case decisions in essence served to amend our great Constitution by judicial fiat, as opposed to the Constitution's own carefully drawn procedure, which requires a two-thirds vote of the people through their legislative representatives (state or national). Once the people allow such "amendments" without a public outcry—in fact providing public *consent* (even if through ignorance as opposed to true acceptance)—then the initial stage for decline of all our Constitutional Liberties has been set.

The time has come for "We the People" to stand up and fight. No more should we feel constrained to sit idly by and watch these offenses. The Constitution itself provides for a remedy: *impeachment.* We need not wait for Supreme Court justices—or other rogue judges on a liberal rampage to rewrite our history and our government—either to die or to retire of their own volition. These direct and unconstitutional assaults upon our republic are grounds for impeachment. In *The Federalist Papers,* Alexander Hamilton explained the Constitution's key limit on the justices' lifetime tenure:

"All judges who may be appointed by the United States are to hold their offices *during good behavior*" (emphasis in the original).[26] I know we have yet to see Congress implement this constitutional power to impeach judges, but that does not mean such power is defunct. Isn't it time we voted out congressional representatives who are more concerned with maintaining their position as career politicians than they are with their oath of office to uphold the Constitution of the United States?

With that in mind, the responsibility for halting the decline of America falls upon the shoulders of each and every citizen dwelling safely within its borders. As long as we allow judges to throw off their constitutional restraints and implement an activist interpretive methodology, our republican form of government—and it is just that, a Republic and not a pure Democracy—teeters on a precarious and fragile foundation. We must cease our apathetic acceptance of the judiciary's daily assault upon our liberties.

Each of us has to decide whether we will take a stand in the voting booth and defend our constitutional liberty from constant erosion or continue to send leaders to Washington who will deny the existence of such liberty. Which course will you choose? Originalist justices such as Antonin Scalia need not be in the minority. Rather, by constitutional mandate, such should be the caliber of every justice allowed to serve upon our Supreme Court. Only by electing courageous congressional representatives will we be able to guard our Constitution, as well as the charter document that is its basis, the Declaration of Independence, against erosion and attack from within. Then they will continue to function as the foundation of our liberty they were intended to be.

If we allow the Courts to continue down this path of unbridled attack on our Constitution, then we will ultimately see the rewriting of every one of our amendments to the point of its being unrecognizable. The First Amendment has already been reviewed and redefined so thoroughly as to deny those rights intended to be protected and protect rights that our Founders would have viewed as unlawful establishments. This perversion of our First Amendment rights has become so widely accepted that it has woven its way through the basic fiber of our society.

Similarly, separation of church and state is declared with such force that even those who know its fallaciousness do obeisance to it. Rather, what the cry should be is, "No establishment!" While the campaign continues to destroy any last shred of remembrance of our Christian heritage, carried out by organizations such as the ACLU and people like Barry Lind with Americans for Separation of Church and State, our society at large has overwhelmingly embraced an all-pervasive establishment in its purest form. This unconstitutional establishment has served to help rewrite our nation's history and is an institution even the boldest of souls fears to attack. Its inappropriateness within the sphere of civil authority is becoming pronounced by rampant problems that make it similar to a war zone. This unconstitutional establishment will never solve its problems until it is taken away from the authority of the civil government and given back to the authority of the family.

Chapter Ten

THE ESTABLISHMENT

THE MODERN SUPREME COURT HAS SO
rewritten our Constitution it is no longer
discernible as the great protector of our liberties that the Founders envisioned. The perversion has
been so complete it has protected as rights those things
which our Founders perceived society should denounce,
all the while trampling underfoot the liberties for
which they freely sacrificed their lives. Prayer, the Ten
Commandments, and any mention of God are ostra-
cized from civil society on the premise of separation of
church and state. A cursory review of the Constitution

quickly reveals a distinct absence of any such prohibitive language. The actual language to which the courts inevitably refer is that of the "no establishment" clause.

Documents contemporaneous to the ratification of our Constitution verify the Founders' intent with the inclusion of such language. James Madison, known as the Father of our Constitution because of his extensive involvement in its drafting, also wrote the Constitution for the Commonwealth of Virginia. There, he expounded upon the word *religion* as it was included and defined in Article I, Section 16. *Religion* was defined as our "duties owed to God." In Madison's estimation, such duties being owed to a higher Authority trumped any and all control by civil government. These duties also were expected to permeate every walk of life. The "no establishment" clause was intended to affirm the preemptive authority of obligations occasioned to the Creator of the universe to be superior to that of civil authority. In essence it was a declaration of "o Jurisdiction" or, in layman's terms, "Government, hands off!" to the citizens of this great nation.

Madison and his fellow Framers, in clearly understanding this chain of authority, delineated a boundary beyond which civil government was never intended to extend. Such a trespass as we have seen should be viewed for what it is: an unlawful usurpation of jurisdiction. And, consequently, it is condemned by the supreme law of the land, our Constitution. This interpretation is the only one consistent with both the words and deeds of the Founders. To draft the Constitution, see it ratified by the colonies, and empower Congress to make its first official act, that of appointing chaplains, is completely incongruous if one accepts the interpretation of the modern-day court. If, however, one accepts that the Founders viewed the "duties owed to God" as so inviolable that any establishment vested with power to impede one's ability to abide by the "Laws of Nature and of Nature's God" must be prohibited, then their words and actions make sense. History, contemporaneous documents, and the Constitution itself bear witness to this as truth. After his election as president, George Washington wrote to the United Baptist Churches of Virginia that, "If I could have entertained the slightest apprehension that the Constitution framed by the Convention, where I had the honor to preside, might possibly endanger the religious rights of any ecclesiastical Society, certainly I would never have placed my signature to it."[27] How much more proof do you need than this direct and clear statement from our First President?

Armed with this understanding, we can see that much of what the Supreme Court has attempted within the last fifty years to pass as law amounts to nothing more than insubordination of the Constitution through unlawful amendment. Perhaps what concerns me more than the blatant attempts to deny the church in America its heritage and its rights is the success of extreme indoctrination through acceptance of an all-pervasive establishment.

First, the general acceptance of the doctrine of separation of church and state is very disconcerting in and of itself. A perfect example of this perversion is that of the case against the Ten Commandments monument erected by Alabama's Judge Roy Moore. This monument is not only a historically accurate reminder of the law which was the foundation of all law as viewed by our Founders, it is also an action in compliance with obedience to the constitutionally recognized supreme authority of the Laws of Nature and of Nature's God. The Constitution, through the doctrine of incorporation, by reference undergirds rather than circumvents that of the Declaration of Independence. The unalienable right to worship the Creator according to the dictates of one's conscience was unquestionably included among these rights. The very fact that such rights were included within the First Amendment in order to promote ratification of the Constitution as a whole is further proof that this was a generally acknowledged and protected right, and one of greatest concern, especially to those entrusted with drafting the document.

How then can Judge Moore's historically accurate and constitutionally protected monument rise to the level of an establishment? Further, it is of extreme relevance that this monument was in no way forced upon the masses-at-large through forced participation and support in the way of tax dollars. Judge Moore placed this monument within the public building at his own expense. However, I feel secure in pointing out that were financial support obtained as tax dollars, it still could in no way rise to the level of a constitutionally infringing establishment. This is evident by the Founders' acknowledgement of the superior authority of and duty owed to the Supreme Creator of the Universe. Yet Judge Moore's actions are labeled and routinely accepted as proscribed by the Constitution.

However, while such widespread ignorance of constitutional purity is disheartening, it is not the separation doctrine's establishment to which I refer. Rather, it is that of another institution created, supported, and revered by our society that has developed such pervasive tentacles as to make it virtually impossible to extricate ourselves from it. Further, the very mention of its inappropriateness occasions such gasps and whispers of heresy as to make the bravest of men of conviction faint with apprehension. Perhaps it is immaturity that makes me bold, or perhaps it is the motivation of a greater concern for the coming generations, but I am about to tread upon an area deemed as sacred to most within the general populace of these United States.

Revelation of the true meaning and intent of the Founders with respect to the No Establishment Clause paints a clear depiction of an institution infringing upon the preeminent source of all authority. The picture reveals an institution that is, to use the words of the modern-day Supreme Court to its own detriment, excessively entangled[28] with that of the civil government. One could concede that the extreme of such entanglement would be state-mandated support through taxation. The model establishment would then be that of a tax-supported institution that instructed citizens in a belief system that impacted a great majority of the populace as a whole and coerced and mandated support by the sword of governmental authority rather than by free will. Is this ringing any bells to anyone yet? If not, it is because such an institution has become so safely insulated behind a cloak of public good and benefit as to become immune of criticism.

The irony is that it is the very fine line between good and evil that makes this institution so dangerous. The enemy has for generations used the same tactic of disguise by publicizing the good to be found within the fruit of enticement so as to shroud the bitter price to be paid in the end. To allow the creation of such an institution would be to ultimately allow the beginning of the end, to create a vehicle for propaganda and imposition of an improper worldview, all the while replacing the belief system espoused by the Founders who sacrificed to purchase our liberty. It soon becomes a liberty we find ourselves unknowingly surrendering to those powers yielding the hand of control over this establishment.

While we have been taught to accept the white elephant of establishment and even embrace it within society, we are simultaneously told by the courts that those elements viewed by the Founders as beyond the control of civil authority are in fact the sources of establishment. We are truly living in an upside-down kingdom where good is deemed evil and evil is touted as good.

IDENTIFYING THE ESTABLISHMENT

Our clues come from answering a series of questions. First question: Where are citizens taught that they owe a higher duty of allegiance to the state than to God, as evidenced by their mandated avoidance of any mention of God within this institution? I realize this clue hits too many establishments to allow any one major offender to be isolated. Second question, then: Where is a large portion of the general populace daily instructed in the religions of secularism, humanism, evolution, and so on? Third question: Which institution derives it financing from taxation irrespective of one's acceptance of the belief systems and religious philosophies expounded therein? Final question: What institution is so entangled with civil authority as to make its extrication practically impossible, since it would seal the doom of its very existence? There is one answer to all the above questions. It is the public education system.

One need not wonder long why the enemy chose such a subtly deceptive tool of perversion. Remember the adage mentioned above, that the students of one generation will become the leaders of the next. Even secular society has discerned the power derived through modifying the thoughts and behaviors of a generation. Not only is such control powerful, but it is also very difficult to turn the tide, to undo the damage done. If a worldview becomes consistently accepted, then the deception grows exponentially. This battle for our nation's children and who will control their education and training is crucial to our success for reclaiming our nation. Consider this quote from an eleven-year-old student attending a private Christian school:

> Why did the Pilgrims come to America in the first place? Why? Clearly it was to have the freedom of religion. The founder of the state of Rhode Island, the missionary Roger Williams, founded this state so that we could truly have freedom of religion. One of the first books to be printed in America was a Bible translated by Jim Elliot, to minister to Indians.[29] So numerous were those led to the Lord that they were soon called *"Praying Indians"*, at least they were called that after he taught them the Word of God. Our Founding Fathers would be mortified to see that the country for which they sacrificed their lives came to such a lowly

place as this, as to lie about our Constitution and to even suggest that this country was not founded on Christian principles. In simpler words when one is using the debate of Church and State they are truly using a debate of error.

Can you imagine such a statement freely being made by a student in a public middle school? Do you now understand why it is so crucial to the enemy's success to inhibit and even prohibit the instruction of truth to our nation's children? Our children are, after all, our best and greatest assets, and we are throwing them into the enemy's flames even as the children of Israel threw their children to Moloch.[30]

I would venture to guess that many reading this book, although it is intended solely for instruction of the body of Christ, are finding its content foreign and extreme. I have perceived that familiarity breeds comfort far more often than it does contempt. If someone is told often enough that something is good, it feels awkward the first time he or she comes in contact with a voice decrying such good to in fact be evil. I may be the first voice telling you that surrendering to the civil government our familial jurisdiction over our children is a dangerous and unconstitutional path to tread. I realize such an argument may seem foreign, but I believe it to be true just the same. Truth has never needed the masses' consent to remain true.

I also perceive the world will always be in opposition to truth. Truth exists in the person of Jesus Christ, and anyone who denies Him is a foreigner to truth. Jesus said, "I am the way the truth and the life..." (John 14:6). Why should we be shocked that the general masses have difficulty accepting truth when they deny the very person of truth? As believers, the Holy Scriptures, the very embodiment of Christ Jesus, must be our objective standard of truth in every area of our lives.

Even if you question the accuracy of my constitutional interpretation as proof of the inappropriateness of a state-created, tax-payer supported school system, still the Scriptures bear witness to such an institution's lack of proper authority in the life of the Christian family. It was compliance with scriptural truth that motivated all the efforts of the Father of our great nation. In his farewell address, President Washington called his country to correct any defects he may have occasioned, saying, "Whatever they may be I fervently beseech the Almighty to avert or mitigate the evils to which they may tend. I shall also carry with me the hope that my country will never cease to view them with indulgence; and...with an upright zeal, the faults of incompetent abilities will be consigned to oblivion."[31] His intent being clear, even assuming a failure on the Founders' parts to accomplish this intent, compliance with scriptural truth would be the fulfillment of their wishes and the proper response of a society so indebted to their contributions. It would be our obligation then, as their successors and heirs, to ensure that our government continued to function within the proper parameters as supported by the Holy Scriptures.

Where does the Scripture address the establishment of public schools? It is contained in the question of jurisdictional authority, as explained in Chapter 4. The authority for instruction of children resides securely within familial jurisdiction, and therefore God clearly holds parents responsible, not the state. For the state to usurp this authority and responsibility, whatever its good intentions, is to operate outside the parameters of proper jurisdiction. Power devoid of authority rises to the level of tyranny; therefore, such actions by the state are clearly tyrannical. This activity has become so pervasive that the government mandates our support of this institution, irrespective of our individual beliefs, acceptance, or even participation in the government-sponsored education. Many states require complete obeisance to the civilly established institution, requiring parents to seek permission from the civil authorities prior to instructing their own children. This is true for private and parochial schools' need for compliance and, even more extensively, for parents to instruct their children at home. This is clearly in defiance of the intent of the Founders to foster compliance with the Laws of Nature and of Nature's God.

As noted earlier, the ancient Greeks' doctrine of *parens patriae* postulated that the civil government was the ultimate parent of every child, and as such held ultimate authority over all the children in the state. This doctrine is no different from that evidenced by our state legislatures, who draft laws detailing their belief in the state's supreme authority and delegating to parents only that authority which they will allow them to possess. This belief system is the basis for compulsory education that dictates to the parents and usurps familial authority beyond civil jurisdiction.

If you doubt for one moment that public schools infringe upon our constitutional freedoms, you need look no further for proof than the abridgment of students' rights found in the wake of judicial activism. Federal court decisions denying students their constitutional right of Free Exercise are replete and all based upon the underlying religion of secularism. Secularism is by definition a belief system, and one that denies the existence of a Supreme Being. "Secularism is unconstitutional... preferring those who do not believe over those who do....[32] [T]he State may not establish a 'religion of secularism' in the sense of affirmatively opposing or showing hostility to religion, thus preferring those who believe in no religion over those who do believe." Therefore, to tout secularism as the standard within the walls of our public schools is to further underscore this institution as an establishment of a religion. The creation of an establishment necessitates the revocation of the free-exercise clause. Students across our nation are required to leave their constitutional freedom to worship according to the dictates of their consciences outside the schoolhouse. This is a necessary evil. However, you don't even get to this point if you accept that education is a familial obligation and one that should be addressed by the civil authority only where it exists on a strictly voluntary basis with the family delegating authority to the state and not the other way around. This can be done, as schools were not initially tax-supported but, rather, community-supported on a volunteer basis from participating parents. Traditionally, education in the Western world has been planned, organized, and provided by the church. Moreover, the education children received revolved around the Scriptures, and the God whom they reveal.

While this concept may at first seem foreign to you, my prayer is simply this, "You shall know the Truth, and the Truth shall set you free." God has never needed nor required a majority. He is seeking, as usual, a remnant of a faithful few. It is through the faith of these saints the Lord may confound the wisdom of this world. The world does not comprehend the strategy of the Father, nor can they, for, as the apostle Paul wrote, "[O]ur struggle is not against flesh and blood, but against the rulers, against the authorities, against the powers of this dark world and against the spiritual forces of evil in the heavenly realms" (Eph. 6:12). We must also be shrewd in this warfare and be reminded that our weapons are not carnal but mighty through the pulling down of strongholds (2 Cor. 10:3-4).

While all of the above is an idealistic approach, on a practical note, however, it would not be wise, nor even feasible, to do away with the public education system. We have too many families and students who are wholly dependent upon it. The only real and viable change that can be made at this point is to reintroduce competition into the equation. As Americans, we understand the positive power and influence of competition. Competition drives the free-enterprise system and sees those able to fulfill a need most effectively as the ones who succeed. Competition, therefore, forces everyone to do their very best, to earn customers. Regrettably, this is the ingredient that has been taken out of the monopoly of public education.

We need to allow parental choice to be the driving force behind educational improvement. When schools are forced to compete for your sons and daughters as their students, then schools will rise to the occasion to be their very best. Currently, there is no competition and it is the students who suffer. We must stand unified as the body of Christ on this issue in order to see it have the impact it should have. I understand all the reasons why we should fear tax credits as the means whereby the federal and/or state governments can have their hands in the educational mix once again. However, it is not merely a semantic difference to say the answer should be tax exemptions. Simply put, tax credits are viewed as the government's monies it gives back to you, while tax exemptions are areas in which the government has no right to tax you.

These kinds of subtle but honest distinctions help us as believers choose where we should stand on the issues. The Bible, should we really want to know the answers, has them for every issue known to man. So, what is the answer concerning how we fight to preserve our great nation?

The Father has revealed the key to victory in this present warfare; it lies in the ministry of accountability. Too often we are chastised about our failures only to have the one chastising fail to provide any means of restoration. In this book, I have chastised to convict, not condemn, and I know the Father promises to always provide a means of escape. Victory is assured when we walk according to revelation, that is, the Lord's revealed will. I would like to extend a ray of hope through revelation in the final chapter. Won't you be one of the chosen few to walk this path of restoration?

Chapter Eleven

WATCHMEN ON THE WALL

———➤●◄———

I REALIZE I'VE SPENT A LOT OF TIME DETAILING some of the major problems with our society. The good news is that God never reveals a problem for which He doesn't provide a solution. The Scripture is clear about the importance of the ministry of accountability. It arises from the principle that those who know the truth bear the ultimate responsibility of decrying the consequences of sin.

Ezekiel 33 paints a vivid picture of approaching judgment for the nation of Israel. The chapter also shows that some are aware of the impending judgment; in this case, it was the prophet Ezekiel. This situation exactly parallels that of our present-day society. We, like Israel, are extremely blessed among the nations. The Lord has abundantly blessed us, yet we as a nation have turned our back on Him. We have taken Him out of our schools, out of our government, and out of our lives.

A person's strong commitment to God often gives rise to extreme feelings. When the media describes a person as a polarizing figure, it often serves to confirm that person's genuineness in commitment to the Savior. At best, the elite media cringe at the mere mention of God. At worst, outspoken faith more often elicits extreme hatred. This conflict echoes the ultimate battle between good and evil that has been waged since the beginning of time between Satan and his hordes and God and the angelic host. This hatred is most noticeable at the extremes, between those who knowingly choose the side of good and those who choose its antithesis.

But there are those who believe they are not part of the conflict. They do not realize that those who are not with God have chosen the side of Satan. In a war of this magnitude, no one is exempt; whether one knowingly chooses their allegiance is irrelevant. Unfortunately, a significant segment of society has determined that they are on neutral territory. This "gray area," which the

Scripture calls being lukewarm, is most likely where the bulk of America's population tries to reside. They are those persons not adamantly opposed to God, perhaps even admitting to a vague belief in God, but who have no real personal relationship with Him. They shun a belief system that stringently adheres to His Word as being narrow-minded and intolerant, believing that a human being simply has a responsibility to do good and be good. These are the highest ideals in a world without God.

The Scriptures, though, place these lukewarm persons on the side of evil, and their fate is sure. Though they constitute the majority in our culture, God promises to spew them out of His mouth (Rev. 3:15-16). These who straddle the fence unwittingly make an alliance with the powers of darkness through their unwillingness to seek God with their whole heart. They seek instead to be masters of their own fate and to redefine God, as well as good and evil, through socially evolving standards.

Rather than acknowledge God as God, they fashion a God in their own image, mutilating the Scriptures to support their claims. God, however, proclaims a judgment on anyone who adds to or takes away from His Word. Yet society today arrogantly proclaims that even the God of the Bible must evolve. Believing majority rule is the standard, God's enemies in our society suggest they understand the character traits of omnipotence, omniscience, holiness, justice, and mercy better than God does.

The further one moves along the continuum from the vast abyss of gray closer to either of the polar positions of black or white, the more "polarizing" one becomes in the estimation of the lukewarm. Those who are content to be apathetic in their faith along with those of little or no faith are rarely an offense. However, those who have a strong belief in absolutes and rights or wrongs are highly offensive. For example, when one vehemently holds to the position or belief that killing of innocent babies in the womb is murder, or conversely that a mother should be able to kill any baby that is growing within her womb, the middle people will always take offense. After all, the lukewarm position is to avoid the moral question altogether by taking the position of compromise, e.g., to personally believe abortion is wrong but that government doesn't have a right to impose upon anyone's personal beliefs. The errors of this argument aside—and they are numerous—this is a coward's position. To allow an issue of such moral magnitude as the sanctity of human life to be skirted by political correctness is reprehensible. However, such a position rarely offends the great majority of the public. It is the less polarizing position.

What is my point? Simply this, the closer you get to God and His principles of holiness, or conversely, to Satan and his principles of licentiousness, the more polarizing you are going to be. When you believe in absolutes, you of necessity define what is good and what is evil; there is no more relativism, no neutrality. If, then, you believe in absolutes and you define what is right, then the opposing position is by definition wrong. And those on the side of wrong will loathe you. This is why people such as George W. Bush find themselves loathed. They believe in absolutes because they are devout Christians, and if you are truly a devout Christian, you must believe in the absolutes defined in the Word of God. If you are reading this book and saying to yourself that you are a Christian but you don't believe in absolutes, you deceive yourself. You cannot have it both ways. Jesus put it this way, "No one can serve two masters; for either he will hate the one and love the other, or else he will be loyal to the one and despise the other."

What, then, is our responsibility to our nation? If the United States is like the nation of Israel described in Ezekiel 33, then it is clear we as the church in America have been failing in our duty to warn of impending judgment. Consider how many prayer meetings have included the promise of 2 Chronicles 7:14? There, God explains the terms without equivocation: "If my people, who are called by my name, will humble themselves and pray and seek my face and turn from their wicked ways, then will I hear from heaven and will forgive their sin and will heal their land."

First of all, it is important to note that God is not speaking to the nation as a whole. The healing of the land is dependent solely upon the actions of God's people, not the unsaved. The non-believer can choose either to repent or not repent, and it will have no bearing on what ultimately happens in our nation. What is relevant is what God's people do. Thus far, we have chosen to be disengaged and to disregard our biblical mandate for social involvement. We have failed to use biblical truth as the standard by which we warn our society to turn from its wickedness. Therefore, the Lord requires the blood at our hands, and we dare not take our responsibility lightly. Isaiah 59 tells us that God shuts his ears to hear because of the blood on his people's hands.

Until the body of Christ ceases to compartmentalize their lives into spiritual and secular realms, there will never be a change. Such compartmentalization is rampant and a symptom of a very sickly body. Christians attempting to attain salvation and yet live their lives no differently from anyone else around them can never be used of God to transform our lost and dying world. Examples of such "Sunday Morning Only" Christians are everywhere, and they are the ones who defend supporting political issues or the candidates who hold opinions that are blatantly contrary to the Word of God. I fully anticipate that we will always have lukewarm parishioners in our midst; however, what is even more disheartening is the number of pastors who proclaim from the pulpit that it is not a party issue. Anyone who makes such a ludicrous statement is like the person who babbles that they personally don't approve of abortion but do not feel that the government has a place protecting innocent life. These statements could only be made by persons ignorant of biblical law and are attempts to be politically correct and to avoid offending anyone. The truth in the Scriptures will always be an offense. Anyone attempting to avoid this offense will by extension succeed in avoiding truth.

Ezekiel tells us that our failure to hold society accountable for its actions by warning it of its error places society's blood on our hands. As mentioned above, Isaiah 59:1-3 tells us that this blood on our hands keeps the Lord from hearing our cries. Until the church in America rises up and corrects this situation, we can't even begin to implement the call for healing detailed in 2 Chronicles. The time for action has come and almost gone. It is the eleventh hour and the Lord is waiting to see what the Body of Christ within our nation will do. Will we continue with business as usual, tickling our ears and justifying sin? Or will we lift up the standard of holiness that God expects from His children in all areas of life and proclaim truth from the rooftops?

Chapter Twelve

LESSER CIVIL
MAGISTRATES

————⫘⧫⫘————

I CAN JUST IMAGINE SOMEONE READING THIS book for the first time. Perhaps your spirit is able to receive everything you are reading, but you are asking yourself, "Okay, how do I warn society in order that the blood is no longer on my hands?" There are many different ways to accomplish this task. For example, if you are the pastor of a church, I encourage you to not shrink back from engaging in the social and spiritual warfare that is going on around you. Speak to the issues of the day. Address abortion; address homosexuality; address the need for righteousness in our political leaders. And if this includes hitting hard along party lines, which it should, then render unto Caesar that which is Caesar's and unto God that which is God's.

While I realize most reading this book will not be pastors, I know all are lesser civil magistrates. The common law on which our laws were founded depended on the idea of lesser civil magistrates. This belief posited that within a society all the citizenry held authority. If and when the governing authorities were not operating within their correct realm of jurisdiction, either by doing something they shouldn't or not doing something they should, then the authority shifted from the official to the people. It became the duty and responsibility of the people, as lesser civil magistrates, to hold such official accountable.

Are we responding to our officials and to society as a whole as though we were lesser civil magistrates vested with authority? The situation we find ourselves in today has always posed a threat should the evil find the righteous asleep. We can say with Samuel Langdon, the thirteenth president of Harvard, "We have rebelled against God. We have lost the true spirit of Christianity, though we retain the outward profession and form of it... By many, the Gospel is corrupted into a superficial system of moral philosophy, little better than ancient Platonism... My brethren, let us repent and implore the